MW00737577

Valinda, Our Daughter

Autographed by the author

Gladys Taylor

Gladys Taylor
Duncan, Alta.

Detselig Enterprises Ltd.
Calgary, Alberta

Valinda, Our Daughter

© 1993 Gladys Taylor

Canadian Cataloguing in Publication Data

Taylor, Gladys, 19**
  Valinda, our daughter

  ISBN 1-55059-51-0
  1. Leonard, Valinda Uffelman   2. Victims
of terrorism—Canada—Biography.   3.
Hostages—Canada—Biography.   4. Hijacking
of aircraft—Egypt—Case studies.   I. Title.
HE9882.7.Z7H56   1993   364.1'54'092
                              C93-091510-0

Detselig Enterprises Ltd.
210, 1220 Kensington Road NW
Calgary, Alberta T2N 3P5

All rights reserved. No part of this book may be reproduced in any form or by any means without permission in writing from the publisher.

Printed in Canada   ISBN 1-55059-51-0   SAN 115-0324

Dedicated to the people of Beiseker, Alberta who gathered "as if with outspread arms to hold them" while they said goodbye to Valinda and her baby.

To the memory of Valinda June Uffelman Leonard
and her infant son, Andrew Jarrett

Contents

Author's Acknowledgements:

My gratitude to Valinda's schoolfriends, Shelly (Schmaltz) Schneider, Sheila Fischer, Cathy (Howden) Reboul and Cindy Ternes for sharing their loving memories. Also helpful was Lucille Taylor, whose daughters Valinda lived with in Calgary, and Harvine Gilberg, Valinda's maternal grandmother, who filled me in on the historical background of the family. But most of all my deepest gratitude to the immediate family, Edward Leonard and Leah and Harvey Uffelman.

This book would not have been possible without the inspiration and devotion of Leah. She started it all by not wanting her daughter to be forgotten and she has been with me every inch of the way since, making sure that this book does keep the memory of Valinda and Andrew alive.

Most personally I thank my son, Lorne Taylor, for his help with the Malta research. I could never have gotten the pre-trial transcripts on which I based much of the book had it not been for him.

Finally, there are all the people of Irricana and Acme and the surrounding farms who expressed their sympathy and love in a dozen different ways, all of them reflected in these pages.

Publisher's Acknowledgements:

Financial support for Detselig Enterprises Ltd. 1993 publishing program is provided by the Department of Communications, Canada Council and The Alberta Foundation for the Arts, a beneficiary of the Lottery Fund of the Government of Alberta.

Credits:

Cover artwork by Dean MacDonald
Edited by Sherry Wilson McEwen

Prologue

No one is an island.

Least of all was Valinda Uffelman Leonard an island.

The lifestream that was hers had been nurtured in many and distant places. In Russia, Sweden, Argentina, United States and finally Canada where she grew up on the sun-steeped prairies of Alberta.

The heart that was hers was stilled by terrorists in Malta.

She could have been your daughter.

She could have been mine.

Saturday Night

It was a rainy Saturday night when Valinda's Greek friends drove her and her baby son Andrew to the Athens Airport.

Saturday night has a special significance to all prairie farm girls and Valinda was no exception. It is the night you meet your boyfriend in town or if you haven't a steady boyfriend, it is the night you borrow your father's half-ton and you and your girlfriends go cruising. And if this is really going to turn into a special night you may see the boy you've been secretly dreaming about leaning against a storefront and trying to look as though he isn't interested. After you pick him up, your girlfriends spot someone they like and before long you're having a Saturday night party.

Valinda loved Saturday-night-running-into-Sunday-morning parties. She was looking forward to one of those parties once she and Ed met in Dhahran.

Only a plane flight separated them.

Preface

Valinda and Omar should never have met. Valinda was an ordinary girl who had lived most of her 27 years in a peaceful country subjected to nothing more un-Canadian than the usual veneer of American music, movies and books. She was brought up to love and be loved. The main influences in her life were parents, teachers, friends and the United Church minister.

Omar had lived almost as many years as Valinda but not in a peaceful country. His had been a hot-house atmosphere, maturing him beyond his years. He had probably heard his share of pop songs, even seen the same American movies as Valinda but his real entertainment was too often a cacophony of screams and rifle fire. From his cradle he was taught to hate. He was ingrained with the determination to change his world. The strongest influences in his life were undoubtedly Yasser Arafat, then Abu Nidal, who led a renegade splinter group, including Omar, away from Yasser Arafat's Al Fatah. Omar was born to kill.

The only thing they ever shared was the same plane for 24 hours in a country neither of them had ever seen before. What cruel twist of fate could have brought these two such disparate young people to end up facing each other down the blood-soaked length of a plane?

It is possible that, all unsuspecting, the nine-year-old girl and the four-year-old boy had begun their march to destiny on a June day in 1967 when the headlines around the world screamed, ISRAEL SMASHES ARABS IN SIX DAY WAR. At the end of that war Moshe Dayan told his soldiers, "We have returned to the holiest of our holy places, never to depart again" and with those words unleashed a river of hate and death that is still flowing.

It also triggered an epidemic of hijackings. "Air borne piracy," as it was then called, began the following year. On August 31 a Rome-Tel Aviv flight was taken over by Arab nationalists and forced to land in Algiers. The hijackers called themselves the Popular Front For The Liberation of Palestine. They immediately released passengers of various nationalities but detained 21 Israelis and the crew. In return for the release of their hostages they demanded the release of Palestinian commandos held by Israel since the Arab-Israeli War of 1967.

Six months later in February, 1969, another El Al Jet was hijacked by the Arabs and six passengers wounded. This appears to be the final hijacking under the joint leadership of Arafat and Nidal. In August of 1969 a TWA jet was brought down in Damascus. The Syrians freed all but the Israelis and hijackers.

Hijacking broke out in earnest in 1970 when, within a matter of days, three terrifying headlines appeared in the Jordanian press:

ARAB COMMANDOS HOLD 150 HOSTAGES IN DESERT
ON TWO N.Y. BOUND JETS.

ARAB GUERRILLAS HIJACK BRITISH JET BRINGING
HOSTAGE TOTAL TO 300

ARABS BLOW UP THREE JETS AFTER REMOVING PAS-
SENGERS, FREE 260, HOLD 40

Arab commandos had hijacked and/or destroyed a total of five planes during this period. They had destroyed three in the desert and one in Cairo. Most of the passengers were released but some 50 of them, from five countries – United States, Israel, Britain, West Germany and Switzerland – were held at gunpoint in the stifling heat of the Jordanian desert by terrorists of the Popular Front For the Liberation of Palestine.

A vicious terrorist pattern seemed to be forming although for the next five years other targets than airlines were favored. This redirection of terrorist activity could have been the result of the "hijacking screen" being developed by concerned pilots and their airlines. By January 1973, baggage inspections, including the use of X-rays, were obligatory at airports around the world.

Although these new procedures may have given the airlines a respite, it didn't stop the carnage. Most shattering was the massacre of 11 Israeli Olympians in Munich. The event which proved that "no place is sacred in the gruesome conflict between Arabs and Israelis" was the seizure of an Israeli school by Arabs in which 26 children were killed. In Israel, a bus full of Israeli and Jewish passengers was hijacked. In Athens, Arab gunmen, killed three and wounded 55 in the airport lounge. Eleven years later Omar and Valinda were to leave from that same Athens airport.

In July 1976 the respite from air terror came to a halt with the hijacking of a plane which ended up at the Entebbe Airport in Uganda. Worldwide everyone, including 18-year-old Valinda and 13-year-old Omar, were glued to television sets and radios as the hijacking unfolded. And everyone, except possibly Omar and his friends, drew a collective sigh of relief as word came that "Israeli commandos staged a daring raid to free 105 hostages held by pro-Palestinian hijackers at the Entebbe Airport in Uganda. The terrorists had threatened to start shooting the mostly Israeli and Jewish hostages."

This was the first time commandoes had been called in to rescue passengers. The success of this raid paved the way the following year for another rescue:

West German Commandos stormed a hijacked Lufthansa jet, en route from Majorca to Frankfurt in Somalia and freed 86 hostages just an hour and a half before the terrorists threatened to blow up their plane. All four hijackers were killed.

– Chronicle of the 20th Century. Clifton Webb, ed. Chronicle Publications: Mount Kisco, N.Y., 1987.

In February, 1978, a story that was frighteningly precognitive of what was to happen seven years later read:

Two Arab terrorists shot an Egyptian newspaper editor to death and then the gunmen seized hostages and commandeered a Cypriot airways DC-8. Egyptian commandos tried to storm the plane but 15 of them were killed in a wild shoot-out with Cypriot troops at the Larnaca Airport.

– Chronicle of the 20th Century.

Piece by piece the pattern was forming for Valinda and Omar's hours of hell.

Gladys Taylor
Irricana, Alberta

Other books by Gladys Taylor

Pine Roots
The King Tree
Alone in the Australian Outback
Alone in the Boardroom

Chapter 1

Leah

November 25th, 1985, was Grey Cup Day. In Alberta it was a typical day in early winter. The snow-covered fields stretched to the horizon, their stubble-pocked whiteness reflected in the endless expanse of grey-white sky. It was a day to be remembered for more than football but no one could have guessed it as that day dawned.

I am Valinda's mother, Leah Uffelman. Although it was Grey Cup Day, that Sunday began as most Sundays did on our farm. Harvey and I got up first and had our morning cup of coffee. Vance, our oldest son, who lived in a mobile home across the feed lot from us, was already rousing to start the chores. Harvey would help him later. Verle-Ann, the only other one of our children at home that weekend, was still sleeping. Vaughn and a friend were holidaying in the Canary Islands. Valinda, our eldest, was flying from Athens to meet her husband, Ed, in Dhahran. I was doing my usual "counting off" of my children, a sort of Mother's rosary from my mouth to God's ear.

On weekdays Harvey usually had a farmer's breakfast, bacon and eggs and sometimes potatoes, but on Sundays we generally settled for cereal or toast. This being Grey Cup Day, we had decided to just have coffee. We'd eat a big meal later in the day and in-between, nibble as we watched the game.

Grey Cup was traditionally a fun day for us and our friends. It had become a custom for five couples, who had all grown up together, to gather at one home or another to watch the game. This Sunday the gathering was to be at the Bates' in Acme.

Before we began to celebrate Grey Cup I was going to church. I still attended the little United Church in Beiseker although now the congregation often numbered less than a dozen. This Sunday it was my turn to read the scripture lesson. I was putting on my coat and about to pick up the bible when the phone rang. Harvey answered it.

"You've got to be kidding," I heard him say and saw his disbelieving gaze turn to the *Calgary Herald*. It was lying on the table where we had left it the night before and the headline seared through me just as such headlines had been doing ever since Valinda and Ed had gone to the Middle East. FOUR KILLED AS JETLINER IS HIJACKED.

I sat down quickly on the nearest chair as my mind flashed back to the broadcast of the night before. "I hope Valinda is all right," I had said then, as I always did when something like that was on the news. It had become sort of a talisman to keep her safe. And Harvey had answered as he always did. "Valinda wouldn't be on that plane."

Now, seeing the gray glazed look spreading over his face, I knew the talisman, our secret prayer hadn't worked. Valinda *was* on that plane. Valinda and our only grandson, Andrew. I held the bible tightly and braced myself.

Harvey set down the receiver. "That was the Department of External Affairs, a girl called Jeanette or something . . ." He spoke carefully but without emphasis. "She asked if we had a daughter named Valinda June Leonard. She said Valinda and Andrew were on that plane we heard about last night." The toneless voice droned on. "She said the situation was very controlled. She said she didn't think there was any violence and there was nothing to worry about."

Inside my head the words screamed over and over again. Nothing to worry about, in that terrible part of the world, where the Arabs and Jews are always killing each other, where even now they could be killing Valinda and Andrew? Harvey, reading my thoughts, or perhaps the words were screaming through his mind too, said leadenly, "The girl did say there was nothing to worry about."

"What does she know?" I snapped.

Surprisingly, because he seldom used the living room except when we had company, Harvey walked into the room and sat down in a chair facing the windows.

"She said she would be our contact from now on." His voice was still toneless and terrible.

For awhile we just sat there staring dully out of the window. The sun was trying to shine through heavy grey clouds. "When I fry your eggs in the morning they look just like that yolky sun trying to get through those egg-white clouds," I muttered disconnectedly. Then a little desperately, "We should be doing something, shouldn't we?"

Harvey roused himself wearily, as he sometimes did after a long day in the fields, when it was time to go to bed. "What do you do when something like this happens?" he asked heavily. I had no answer.

We were still looking out of the window when Vance came in from his chores. He saw the look on our faces and stopped in consternation. "What's happened?"

Harvey answered grimly. "We'd better call Verle-Ann. She has to be told too."

Verle-Ann joined us in the living room, still rubbing sleep from her eyes. My heart contracted as I looked at the job-skin covering her head. I had that same dreadful sensation each time I looked at her. Could this be my beautiful child, mutilated before she was 17? Now suddenly I felt another tremor. What if Valinda and Andrew suffered burns like that? What if all my family ended up in job-skins, I thought hysterically.

The truck accident had seemed the worst thing that could ever happen to our family. Verle-Ann had been pinned under the burning vehicle. She'd been fighting her way back ever since. Skin graft after skin graft and she still faced months, probably years of rehabilitation as they tried to replace her ear. But at least she was alive. Valinda might not be that lucky.

"Have you contacted Gordon Taylor?" Vance asked. Gordon Taylor had been our political representative for more years than most of us could remember, first as a Social Credit MLA representing much of the riding my grandfather had once represented and more recently as our Progressive Conservative member in Ottawa.

Thankfully it gave us something to do, some way of holding back our thoughts of Valinda and Andrew on that plane.

"He says he'll see what he can find out and get back to us," Harvey reported after the call. "I'm surprised I got him at the office on a Sunday."

"I'll call Connie," I said. "I have her home number."

Connie Osterman was our MLA. She was also a close friend.

She was as shocked as we were but kept her head. "Try to keep your line open as much as possible," she advised, "so that Ottawa can get through if there's any news."

"She's right," Vance agreed. "But first we should call Ed's folks in Toronto. Maybe they've heard from him."

Before we could get through to the Leonards, Ottawa called again. This time I took the call. After our contact, Jeanette Martin, assured me again not to worry, she added, rather ominously, "The Department would like to suggest that you don't cause too much," she hesitated over the word, "commotion. We don't want to focus the terrorists attention on any one passenger. They may not even know there are Canadians aboard."

I hung up and repeated her words. We looked at each other uneasily.

"Do you suppose they've heard from Gordon Taylor already?" Harvey said. "Is that why they called back so soon?"

"I don't know about Gordon but there's sure as hell something up," Vance said from where he stood at the living room window. "A white van just pulled into the yard."

I recognized the familiar orange-and-white circle symbol on the van. "It's the CBC, Harvey. Do you suppose they can give us some news?" They couldn't. All they did was make me realize that this was real, that half a world away hijackers were threatening my daughter and my grandson.

Vance opened the door with some reluctance. We could see that the CBC crew were already unloading their gear.

"We have nothing to say," Vance warned.

"Of course not. But it's our job to be here," the CBC interviewer said soothingly. He glanced back at his crew. "It's freezing out here . . ."

We had never been inhospitable. Vance let them in. Almost automatically I offered everyone a cup of coffee. I always had coffee on for anyone who dropped in.

Harvey and Vance continued to look wary. The interviewer was obviously seasoned in his job. He had no doubt long since learned that the average family, unaccustomed to the limelight, could be uncomfortable and even hostile on occasions like this. It was his job to gain our confidence.

He and his crew made themselves as inconspicuous as possible while they settled around the kitchen table with their coffee. I found myself wondering where the rest would sit. By now I had no illusions. If the CBC was here, we knew the other stations, the newspapers and the radio people wouldn't be far behind. They weren't. Reporters from local and city papers soon showed up and joined the camera crew in our kitchen.

They all began to talk casually about the weather and who would win the Grey Cup. Harvey and Vance joined them at the table. I went back to the living room, again standing in front of our big windows. I often stood there looking out at the fields stretching beyond the yard's evergreen windbreak. Most often, I stood there when I was waiting for one of the family to come home, although sometimes I just watched the red maple leaf flag whipping about its flagpole. That flag had been my idea, to finish off the setting for our long-planned new home. But there was strain in my shoulders rather than anticipation at a home-coming that day. No, not just strain but anger. Anger in my shoulders, in my whole body, especially in my heart. In sudden fury I scratched on the frost-coated window. The spray of white frost particles hung in the air as I continued to scratch our signal.

I sensed the story-hungry reporter from the *Calgary Sun* looking at me. I knew that before long she would manage to make her way to that window to see what I had scratched. I knew it was her job but it didn't make it any easier. But of course nothing was going to be easy today. I had already begun to fiercely resent the microscopic eyes of the interviewers and reporters now crowding in around my kitchen table.

My table. Our family gathering place. It was on that table that Harvey had perched our little Andrew on his first birthday and we had all looked on with loving eyes as he held his baby court. It was while sitting at the same table, drinking what I now realized could have been my last cup of coffee with Valinda, that we had arranged our signal.

"It's silly, Mother," Valinda had remonstrated with her usual self-assurance. "Nothing's going to happen to me."

"But it could," I persisted. "Suppose you were taken hostage like the people at Entebbe or at the Embassy in Iran. If we had a signal you could let me know if you were all right or if you were being forced to say what your captors wanted. You might even be able to give me a clue as to where you were. What is a word you'd be least likely to say?"

"That's easy." Valinda had laughed, the grammar-conscious schoolgirl in her popping to the fore. "The one word I would never use is 'ain't'. Every teacher I ever had in Beiseker drilled into me the disgrace of saying 'ain't.' I promise you, Mother, if

17

you ever hear me using that word, you can be sure I'm in deep trouble." She was in deep trouble and scratching our signal on the window wasn't going to help a bit.

After awhile Harvey touched my shoulder. He could feel the anger there. Somewhat apologetically he said, "They'd like to take some pictures of us on the couch and ask a few questions. What do you think?"

I nodded and we sat down together. Of course I knew what they wanted. Hadn't I seen scenes like this on TV a hundred times or more? The crew began setting up their equipment. The interviewer tried to draw our attention from the camera by walking to the window and looking out at the fields.

"Is it your land as far as you can see?" he asked Harvey casually.

"Just about. Or it would be if you were looking any direction but that one. That window faces east and our land only goes as far as the highway to the east."

"You have a mixed farming operation, I noticed." He didn't add that the smell of the cattle manure had almost made him sick when he got his first whiff of it. He didn't have to. I had seen the green look on his face as he came in.

Harvey smiled wryly. "The wind must be blowing this way. We don't notice it but sometimes it can get pretty rank."

"Valinda hated that smell." I said involuntarily.

As soon as I said it I realized, with a sinking heart, that I had given the interviewer the opening he had been waiting for. I saw him glance quickly at the cameraman who nodded back reassuringly. He had got it on film. The interviewer moved purposefully back from the window to face us and mentally I shrugged my shoulders. We'd have to give them an interview sometime, it might as well be now.

So, I was ready for the interviewer's first, inevitable question.

"Mrs. Uffelman, when was the last time you saw your daughter?"

When had I last seen my daughter Valinda? When had I ever seen her?

When do any of us, consciously, look at those nearest and dearest to us? Our hearts may bleed for the children in Ethiopia but how often do we see the child beside us fighting for our attention? I didn't want to think of the many times I had brushed off what I thought of as Valinda's capricious demands. I didn't want to think of how seldom I had stopped to consider what might be behind those demands.

I remembered one time when I had popped into the drugstore in Acme, leaving five-year-old Valinda in the car. I hadn't been in the store more than a few minutes before I heard here piping voice demanding, "Is there a mother called Uffelman in here?" How often over the years had she asked that question in a dozen different ways and had I been deaf?

Like so many young brides who conceive in the first year of their marriage, I had been intensely aware of the "new woman" in Harvey's life as soon as she was born. Of course I had been warned this would happen if the baby was a girl but I wasn't prepared for it so soon. I had lost my boyfriend, my lover, too soon. No matter how much I loved her, I also resented her.

And later when everything she did seemed to point up my own inadequacies I resented her more. I remember once talking to her about self-confidence. I thought some of her rebellious behavior stemmed from a lack of confidence. She had turned on me and said, "How can you talk to me about self-confidence when you haven't any yourself?"

Valinda knew how to hurt. And how to shock. During her teens she became less and less popular with the family. She had been going out with a young neighbor. All the family liked him. When Valinda broke up with him, everyone blamed her. Valinda said it was because he couldn't give her the kind of life she wanted. I think she was just trying to say she didn't want to marry a farmer but the family felt she was getting above her station. After all, she was just a farm girl like the rest of them.

Valinda should have had the sense to stay in Calgary until it all blew over. What did she do? She attended the annual church picnic with a new boyfriend, even though she knew the old one would be there. And that wasn't the worst of it. Instead of the usual pants and shirt, she wore a clinging black dress with a slit skirt and cleavage almost to her navel. The family were so angry no one would speak to her. She brazened her way through the day. Just before she left she put her whole pay cheque in the silver collection.

That was Valinda. She had a heart as big as a house. But she was stubborn as a mule and too often it seemed that all her emotions had brass knuckles.

Valinda resented the church orientation on my side of the family. As she said, it was hard being the great-granddaughter of a particularly revered minister who, for forty years, had been the conscience of almost every family she knew.

Yet it was her father's rules that made her the most rebellious. She hated curfews. She hated being an example to her brothers and sisters just because she was the oldest. The only person she seemed to feel truly happy with was her Grandma Uffelman. She liked being the "little Madja" that her grandmother always called her. I think it made her feel small, sweet and secure – all the things she so seldom felt herself to be in the real world.

The family always said that Valinda was searching for something. That, they said, was the only way to explain her wayward nature. I wondered if, in her beloved Greece, she had found what she was searching for? She could have. She wrote once that she felt as though Jesus had walked in Greece as well as Paul. She knew her bible whether she wanted to or not. Maybe she even went back to it.

Valinda loved the song of the birds. Once she said, "I can't bear to think I won't live long enough to hear all the bird songs in the world, see all the flowers in the world and taste the wind off everything, the ocean, the desert, the jungle. Why are we only allowed one time and one place in this world?"

When she went to Greece I think she felt she had managed a second time and place. I suspect she remade herself when she went to Greece – maybe that was why she was so happy there. The brass knuckles were hidden.

If that was what happened, she was lucky. How many of us get a chance to remake ourselves in the way we really want to be? Too often we are foiled in our attempts by the people who can't wait to remind us of what they call "real nature;" the people who won't let us smooth the rough edges, who won't give us a second chance. Had she got that second chance in Greece?

Had she finally regained her little Madja image?

Valinda was not an easy child to raise. And I was not an easy mother to reach. Too often I ran away from closeness, fleeing to the unemotional environment of UCW meetings or Home and

School affairs, even a Toastmistress Club. I think indirectly Valinda sent me to the Toastmistress Club. I was seeking self-confidence. Whether I gained it or not meant little now. It would be no use to Valinda.

When had I last seen Valinda? I started as the reporter repeated his question. In the end, I answered the question the way the interviewer expected me to.

The last time I saw her was in August. We were out in the yard and she and Andrew were getting in the car for Harvey to drive them to the plane. I didn't go. I hate saying goodbye or meeting people at airports. Those places always seem so cold and empty after everyone has gone.

It had been a lovely warm day and I was standing near the flagpole as they left. I stayed there watching until Harvey turned south on to the highway. I lost sight of them for a minute or two but knew I would see them again as they topped the ridge. You could always see cars on the highway when they reached that spot. On a Saturday night Valinda used to watch for her boyfriend's car topping that rise and if he was one Harvey didn't like, she would slip out and meet him before he reached the yard. I waved once more as Harvey's car topped the ridge and disappeared. It was the last time I saw Valinda.

I felt drained after the interview. I sat on the couch and my mother brought me a cup of tea. It was only then I realized that the family had gathered, as they always did in time of trouble: my sister Gloria and her husband Larry Konschuk, my mother, who had come with them, my sister Inga Kronlund and her daughter Lorie. All my family lived within a 10-mile radius. We were a very close-knit family.

Harvey's relatives, the Mervin Goodmans, had also arrived. Like everyone else, they brought food. Food! The universal way to express emotions which were inexpressible. I had carried food many times to my friends. Frances and Wendall Schmaltz, our closest and oldest neighbors arrived, their hands and hearts full as well. Frances hugged me. "She was almost like one of my own," she whispered. I recalled the many afternoons we had spent at the Acme swimming pool watching our children playing in the water while we discussed their grades, their friends, their futures, as all mothers do. Could we ever have envisioned during those happy days, a moment like this?

The afternoon wore on. There was a constant ringing of the phone. So many friends and relatives who had just heard the news and wanted to express their sympathy. I dealt with each one as briefly but as appreciatively as I could. I explained that we wanted to keep the line open for news from Ottawa. I thanked them. My voice broke occasionally. I tried hard not to let it happen often. I tried particularly hard because of the TV and newspaper people waiting so eagerly for some scrap of emotion.

"I've seen too many people on TV breaking down for everyone to watch," I said grimly when Inga asked me how I could do it. "I've watched them lose all their dignity. I won't let that happen to us." I added with finality, "Valinda wouldn't want us to make a scene. She'd hate that."

The Grey Cuppers arrived. They might have watched the game but it was obvious from their strained faces that they hadn't had a party. They kissed me and shook hands with Harvey. "Any news?"

We shook our heads. The calls had kept coming from Ottawa but although we answered them with hope, there had been no more news. I was beginning to hate the words "very controlled," the only ones Ottawa seemed to know.

Joe Clark phoned. He was the Minister of External Affairs. If anyone had additional news, he should have. All he had to offer was his sympathy. And of course he too assured us that "everything was under control." He ended by saying his office would continue to keep in touch with us and presumably with Malta.

Unbelievably, the *Calgary Sun* reporter asked us to stand by the phone for a picture. She wanted us to pose as we had been when we first got the news. She even wanted me to hold my bible. I was furious. How could they ask us to play-act at a time like this? I hoped my look would shrivel her. To break the tension, Inga and Gloria began handing out the sandwiches they had been quietly preparing in the kitchen. There was fresh coffee and some of the baking the friends had brought. I suddenly realized we had not eaten all day. Harvey managed to force down a little and so did I. Inga insisted we eat. "You may need it," she said and I was despairingly aware of what she meant. We didn't know what might still be ahead.

Vance left, supposedly to attend to the cattle again but I knew he was phoning Inga's son, Jimmy. They had a satellite dish and Jimmy was monitoring the American newscasts. We had been switching to and fro from the CBC to CTV. I suspected we were not getting all the news that was being broadcast in the States. The CBC reported that hostages were being killed every 15 minutes and that two Israelis and two Americans had been murdered. When I heard about the Israelis a terrible thought struck me and before I could stop myself I gasped it out. "What if they think Valinda is Jewish! Uffelman could be a Jewish name and it was still on her passport."

No one answered or looked me in the eyes.

When Vance returned his face was white. "They're not telling us all they know," he shouted angrily. "That bunch in Ottawa is just stringing us along with all their phone calls."

Inga made a move to silence him and I understood why. Part of me wanted to know what he had heard but most of me didn't. Once the words I feared the most were said, I could never go back to pretending nothing was happening on that plane.

The day was dying around us. The skies were lowering and shadows filled our home. Mechanically I got up and began switching on lights, delaying the moment.

Vance could hold back no longer. "They've killed all the children," he blurted out and dropped his face in his hands.

The reporters gasped along with everyone else. But their shock was only momentary. A moment later the photographers grabbed their cameras and the TV crews swung their equipment into focus on us. Thankfully, our friends and relatives were too fast for them. As one, they surged forward and surrounded us, their bodies wrapping us lovingly and protectingly from the eyes of the world.

Vance finally broke away and began shouting at the media people. "Get out of here. We don't want you here. Leave us alone." His last words ended in a sob and he turned his face to the wall and wept. The reporters and photographers and TV crews silently left our stricken home.

"Turn off the TV and the radio," I finally pleaded. "I can't bear to hear those words again." By now the Canadian stations were broadcasting the same news Vance had heard earlier over the American stations. With no new details to add, they repeated the same terrible words over and over again.

"All the children on board are dead."

Together we wept for Valinda's son, Andrew Jarrett, the beautiful fair-haired boy who had captured our hearts a few short months before. We recalled the party I had given for his first birthday.

"He blew out the candles and then clapped for himself just as we did," Verle-Ann said tearfully.

Andrew, age one year, at his first birthday party

"Valinda always kept him so nice," Inga recalled. "I'll bet he had on a new outfit when he got on that plane. She'd have dressed him up for Ed's first glimpse of him."

"It's too bad Grandma Uffelman hadn't lived to see him," my mother said. "She was so fond of Valinda, she'd have adored her baby."

"I'm glad my mother never had to live through this," Harvey answered grimly.

Our friends and family stayed on, comforting us with their presence. There was a call from Ed's parents in Toronto. They were coming out.

"We are all Andrew's grandparents," Stan Leonard said. "We should be together at a time like this." He went on, "We're still trying to get through to Ed. I've got my old friend Senator Stan

Haidaz working on it. Stella is going crazy thinking of Ed being alone through all this."

"We've been thinking of him too," Harvey said. "He needs the comfort of a loved voice at a time like this."

Like survivors on a desert island, we needed the comfort of each other.

Our house had gentled now. The anger and resentment which, in our pain, we had begun to focus on the reporters and photographers was gone now that they had left. The grieving could begin. All of us in this room were people who had faced death before: Harvey's parents, my grandparents, my sister Mona. We knew how to handle death. Unbidden, I remembered Mother's story about the two little Irricana girls they had buried many years ago. They were from a Catholic family who were so poor they had no way of getting to Beiseker to attend mass so the people there who might have helped them, knew nothing of them. When the two little girls of the family died, the father, in desperation, came to my grandfather to bury them. The children were so small and undernourished they put them in one coffin. My grandfather made it and my grandmother and my mother and her sisters lined it with pieces of grandmother's white wedding dress. My mother and her sisters carried the little girls to their burying place.

In a minister's family you learned early to deal with death and when there was no one else to bury the dead, you did it. In a minister's family you were exposed to death so often you learned quickly to spread love over the loss and wrap it in layers of memory. But you couldn't begin that process under the prying eyes of strangers, strangers who only wanted to record your emotions for others to see.

Even as I thought those things, I knew our problem was more than the prying eyes. There was something so unnatural about this. All our deaths had been among loved ones, the dying surrounded by the grieving. But this was different. Valinda was alone in her dying, Andrew was alone in his dying. And there was no one there to grieve.

It was then that for me, the denial set in. Was there really dying taking place on that plane? In spite of what was being said, I couldn't, wouldn't believe they were dying. The hope I had nourished from the first moments simply would not die. Valinda must have found a way out of this. She'd always been so resourceful.

"They said they let the Egyptian and Filipina women off the plane. Perhaps one of them hid Andrew under her clothes. He was very small. Valinda would have thought of something like that." I said.

"It would be like her to try something like that," Harvey admitted. "She never gave up easily."

"And the only women they have reported killed are Israelis and Americans," I continued determinedly. At the back of my mind I knew I was wishing for the death of others so my daughter could be safe but I could not help myself. So intense were these thoughts of denial that I was not surprised at the phone call that came next nor at its contents.

It was 10 p.m. and the phone had been quiet for some time. It was now midnight in Eastern Canada. Could the call be from Ottawa at this hour?

Vance answered the phone. After the first few words he almost dropped the receiver in his excitement. "It's the Today Show from New York, Dad. They say they have news of Valinda."

Harvey talked to them and as he did so the grayness receded slightly from his face. "You're sure?" he asked and then motioning for us to give him a pencil, wrote something down. "They say Valinda is alive in a Malta Hospital," he said. "They say she has been trying to reach us. They gave me the number to call." I took the slip of paper with shaking fingers and began to try to place the call. It wasn't as hard as I expected. I reached Malta and then the hospital. "It can't be a hoax," I said, "they gave us the right number."

I started to explain to the person at the other end why I was calling. I hadn't got far when the line went dead. I tried again and the same thing happened. "It's as though they don't want to talk to us," I said in some bewilderment. "But why . . . unless . . . " the unspoken thought hung in the room.

"Give it one more try," Harvey said encouragingly. I looked at the faces of my sisters and mother and knew they were silently praying. Praying just as hard as I was. We were a family accustomed to prayer. It gave me courage to go on.

This time as I made my desperate plea for information about Valinda, the line didn't go dead. A heavily accented voice said, yes, they did have some of the plane victims in that hospital but there was none by that name. I clung to him over the phone. I described Valinda and begged him to go through the wards and see if he could find anyone answering her description. I told him about her odd-shaped toes. When he came back his voice sounded heavier or was it just that the line was jumbled? The hospital was crammed with people, he said. It was hard to find anyone. He went on like that for a moment and then the line went dead. Then I cried.

Chapter 2

Abram

It may have been Grey Cup Day in Canada but in Malta, on the other side of the world, there was death on the runway at Luqa Airport. There the parched crust of the beige earth under the cracked runway waited, as it had been doing since long before the Crusades, to suck up the fresh blood to be spilled.

I, Abram Goldman, was a reporter who happened to be at the airport that November day in 1985. I had come there earlier in the afternoon to see Gilda off on her flight to Israel. I have never been sure why I lingered there that afternoon but in the many nights since when I have wakened with screams in my ears, I have wished I hadn't.

I suspect my newsman's nose had picked up a scent. Nothing the casual observer would have noticed. The clerks were still shuffling papers, the machines still chattering but for me there was a sense of urgency about everything, especially the timbre of the voices, although I hadn't been able to catch any actual words. So I hung around, playing out my hunch.

Eventually all my antennae were screaming. What set them off was that although by now I was sure there was a plane coming in, there were no passengers waiting to board and no relatives and friends waiting to meet those passengers arriving. It was eerie. And yet for me, a Jew, it had not so much eeriness about it as a sense of horror relived. What horror I couldn't guess although my mind, with treacherous trickery, conjured up glimpses of trains speeding across Europe to gas chambers, ships filled with Jews turned despairingly away as country after country refused them sanctuary, all of it wrapped in the Ship of Fools mockery of this plane which I was sure was arriving but which no one seemed prepared to meet.

The minutes ticked by. There were still no plane arrivals flashing on the screen. Finally my mind accepted what had become the obvious in this terrorist-filled year of 1985. Another hijacking!

The airport lights had not been turned on, but the periodic flashes of lightning illuminated the tarmac for electrifying moments. It was during one of these flashes that I got a never-to-be-forgotten glimpse of the plane as it came down. Bathed in a surrealistic glow of bluish light it had the look of the biblical thunderbolts so dear to my forebears.

My forebears, my Jewish heritage. Were any of us ever free of it? Was it my prophet strewn ancestry rather than my news sense that had made me so sure a plane was coming in? I was of a generation of people who had lived most of their lives in a hijacked world. I had even been involved in a hijacking myself. Perhaps that accounted for my sensitivity to what was about to happen. Hijacking of course is but a variation in the weapons that during my people's history has ranged from slingshots and the parting of the seas to Joshua's trumpet and gunpowder and all that has come after. According to historians wars for my people were never-ending, although each generation seemed to have their own benchmark war.

For my generation it was the Six Day War. My mother and I were in the crowd streaming into the walled Old City of Jerusalem after our soldiers had wrested it from the control of Jordan. For the first time in my mother's memory Jerusalem was reunited under Israeli control. She wept. My father, we learned afterward, was weeping in a different way. His blood was weeping into the thirsty soil of the Sinai Desert. He was my personal sacrifice to the age-old war to preserve a homeland for my people.

The only other soil in the world that has drunk more Jewish blood than the Holy Land is the soil of the death camps in Auschwitz and Belsen and dozens of other places where still more of my ancestors have lost their lives. Now the thirsty Maltese soil waited for its blood. I had no doubt some of it would be Jewish.

It seemed to me I had been looking at death for hours. I had lost track of how long it had been since the first body had been tossed out of the plane. From the wireless we heard the pilot's repeated pleas for fuel and the hijacker's continuing threats to kill a passenger every 15 minutes until he got the fuel. We knew the passports had been gathered. We knew there were two

Israeli girls on the plane. So when the dreaded first 15 minute interval had passed and the plane door opened, I knew it would be an Israeli girl they were throwing out. Expecting this, I had wormed my way to a spot as close to the plane as I dared. Not that I imagined I could do anything for her. But perhaps somehow she would know that a fellow citizen shared her terror.

I was close enough to hear her scream. I knew it was the moment when he had first shoved the gun in her face. I could hear the crack of his hand as he slapped her to stop her screams. I heard her shrieking, "No! No!" and the word echoed in my whole being. I saw the flash as the gun was fired. I saw her slump and like a bag of laundry tumble down the flight steps.

In spirit I was with her. I had the emotional scars to prove it. It was barely 18 months since Gilda and I had spent 10 endless hours on a hijacked bus on our way south from Tel Aviv. In my memory I could smell it, I could hear it, I could feel it as if it were yesterday.

There had been thirty-five passengers on that bus and we had been just as stunned as the passengers on the plane must have been when we realized we were being hijacked. The Arabs, armed with explosives, had forced their way on our bus and told us to remain seated and still if we didn't want to be killed.

I remembered the progression of terror as the hours went by, just as the terror must be building on this plane. We on the bus had been fortunate that much of our hijacked time had been during the night, saving us the torment of sitting for hours under a relentless sun. Fortunately for those on the plane, the rainstorm had so far saved them the excruciating discomfort of an enclosed space exposed to Malta's brassy sun.

According to the scraps of conversation we kept hearing over the wireless, the passengers in the plane had been segregated. This was necessary so they could find their special victims, the Israelis. There had been no need for segregation on our bus since we were all Israelis and Jews. But even so they had moved people around, putting the families with children together at the back, moving passengers from other seats they wanted themselves. The seats they wanted were at the front, the centre and the back. That way they could be sure we would all be aware of their weapons and the hopelessness of our position.

The crying of the children had seemed to bother my hijackers the most. They had cast warning looks and made threatening gestures at the mothers. I had been glad Gilda and I had no children. As I saw one woman clasping her child to her breast to keep its sobs from being heard, I recalled another woman of our people who had taken the chance of smothering her baby in just that way in order to save the rest of her party as they hid from the Arabs. The story had been so real to me I could still see the look on the woman's face when, the danger over, she had looked at her baby and realized she had lost the gamble. Her friends were safe but her baby was dead, another victim of our pursuit of a homeland.

They said there were eight children on board. Had they and their mothers been herded to the back? Were they being threatened? There had been a flurry of rumors – all the children had been killed. I didn't believe that – there would have been a shrieking from the plane that the Mothers of Salem couldn't equal. Some of them, though, might have been close to suffocation as their mothers tried to still their cries.

Being at the back the mothers and children would be near the washrooms. Ordinarily it would have been helpful for them to be near the facilities. But I knew from experience that as the hours wore on, the smell could be almost anesthetizing. The toilets would be full, there would be no paper, the floors would be running with urine from nervous men or others too angry at what was happening to care. That was how it had been on the bus.

Worst of all, as the hours dragged on, there were those who would never be able to force themselves to walk down that long aisle of the plane with guns at their backs. Those passengers would prefer to sit in their own excrement. The urine would already be seeping into the seats. The smells would be rising from every corner of the cabin. On the bus we had been allowed to open the windows slightly to relieve the smell. This was impossible on the plane.

And yet despite the smells and the growing terror, some would still be able to sleep, fitfully perhaps but at least it would be sleep. Terror alone would have exhausted them. It had us. Gilda had slept in my arms. At this moment there was probably more resting and a greater measure of comfort on the plane than for we who were keeping watch in the dark. We who were waiting and watching – for what?

On the bus our ordeal had ended shortly after daybreak. We had been released. But could that happen here? I doubted it.

Our Arab captors had, on the whole, been reasonable, even kind people. Surely there could be no reason, much less kindness, in a man who had already executed three people. I hoped the passengers were sleeping because God alone knew what was in store for them.

Chapter Three

Ed

✈ ✈ ✈ ✈

On November 24, 1985 I was in Dhahran, Saudi Arabia, awaiting the arrival of my wife Valinda and son Andrew. They were on a flight from Athens to Cairo. I had arrived a little early so as I sat and waited for the plane's arrival I was quite relaxed. After all I had spent a lot of my time the past couple of years waiting in airports for Valinda. I was used to it. Today I had no book so I ended up daydreaming.

What really had brought me, Ed Leonard, to this far away place and this moment?

My parents, Stan and Stella Leonard had immigrated to Canada from Poland many years ago. I was born in Toronto in 1952 and went to school in Etobicoke prior to attending the University of Toronto where I got a degree in landscape architecture. Since my father was successful in the construction business he had plenty of use for my landscaping skills. I married a Toronto girl and we had a daughter Chloe. We had a close family relationship. My father, mother, two brothers and a sister along with their families and mine spent many happy get-togethers around Dad's new swimming pool. All this ended, for me at least, when my marriage broke up.

My ex-wife and Chloe moved to Calgary and eventually I followed them there so I could spend more time with my daughter. It was in Calgary that I met Valinda, at a Christmas party in 1981. She had a fresh, youthful, wholesome look. But for all her youthfulness I soon found out she was an amazingly capable and mature woman. She was physically strong, probably from carting around all the belongings she insisted on carrying with her whenever she moved. Eventually I realized that her real strength came from her family, true pioneer stock whose roots went back to Europe as did mine.

We were married in 1983 and shortly after I went to Saudi Arabia to work for a company called Agronomics Arabia. While waiting for the job to come through (the red tape was unbelievable) Valinda and I had read all we could about Saudi.

My first job was in Yanbu, an "instant city" created on Saudi's west coast as an industrial centre and shopping depot. There was only one catch about the move to Saudi; I soon found out my job carried only single status and Valinda would have to visit me on temporary visas. Of course my boss promised me I would get changed to married status as soon as possible but in the meantime Valinda had to wait for a visa each time she wanted to visit. The other drawback to our dreams of a rosy future was that Valinda had to leave Canada if we were to benefit from non-resident tax-free status. Because I had two families to support and needed my full salary, this tax-free status made a big difference to our plans.

Valinda was equal to the emergency. She decided she would live in Europe on her own while waiting for the visas. For a girl who had never been out of Canada and only spoke English this should have seemed rather daunting if not downright terrifying. But Valinda never blinked an eye. I was very proud of her and a little amazed when a few months after I left she headed off for Europe alone. She first went to Italy but then, realizing it was too expensive, travelled to Greece. She found an apartment and settled in, all without knowing a soul or having anyone to translate. She was quite a woman.

Yet when she finally did get to Saudi on her first visa she still had all the little girl wonder of a farm kid finding herself for the first time in an exotic world about which she had only read or perhaps seen in movies. For example, she was enthralled to know that among the residences I maintained were two of the King's palaces in Jedda and a palace on the Red Sea for the son of the Crown Prince. The Red Sea. That really rocked her. The first time she saw it she just stood and looked at it. And then she said, "Do you suppose this is where the Red Sea was parted for the Israelites?"

"You've seen too many Charlton Heston movies," I teased.

"I've listened to too many sermons," she retorted. "Have you forgotten my great-grandfather was a preacher for 40 years?"

"No, but you'll have to admit that was before your time."

"Yes, but I still heard a lot of sermons. My mother never missed a Sunday in Beiseker. Anyhow I can just imagine them crossing here."

She couldn't wait to go swimming in what she called "that biblical water."

We made a lot of friends in Yanbu, ex-patriots like ourselves though mostly American. There was only one damper on our good times. Both Valinda and I liked a drink and alcohol was taboo. We were soon making our own wine just as our friends were and as my father did in Toronto. Ours, of course, was only drinkable while his was so tasty he had even given it a brand name.

Things looked good for us in Yanbu. Valinda finally figured out a way to beat the visa problem. She would get a job herself. And she almost did. She applied for a job at the local hospital and they seemed ready to hire her until she took her medical. She was pregnant!

Of course she was disappointed. She had set her heart on working in Saudi and not having to worry about visas anymore. When I twigged her about her attitude she said it wasn't that she didn't want to have children, just not then. As far as I was concerned, I already had a daughter, so it wasn't an urgent matter to me. Needless to say, when we finally saw our son that day in the Athens hospital where he was born neither of us had any regrets. A few weeks later we flew home to Canada to show him off.

By the time Valinda was allowed into Saudi again, I had changed my job. I was now manager of our operations at Riyadh. It was a move up the ladder for me but not a happy move for Valinda. My company had no employee housing in the western compound so we had to live in a poorly-constructed apartment block in a Saudi community. It was small and cramped and hot. And Valinda, who was usually open-minded and eager to meet new people and new cultures, seemed to find the class distinctions, to which she was now exposed each day, unbearable. Particularly the third-class status of women. "They're hemmed in like a bunch of chickens in a cage," she would moan. "I can't bear to think of it."

I would never have called Valinda a free-thinker or a feminist but she had an inborn sense of freedom which I supposed had been fostered by the fact that she had never really wanted for anything in her life. Her family was not rich perhaps but they were very comfortable. She was used to space; her father owned four sections of land and even in Alberta that is a good-sized farm. She had been comparatively free of restrictions since she was 16. She was her own woman.

To end up in Riyadh, one of the most rigid cities in that part of the world, was just too much of a culture shock. Her hatred focused on the *abaya* she was supposed to wear every time she went out. She would be considered "indecent" without it but I think her independent free spirit rebelled at everything she saw. The leers and sneers of the men at her "indecency" without the *abaya*, the subservience of the women peering out from behind their veils, the rules about drinking and a dozen other attitudes they displayed, each infuriated her because she saw these activities as so harmless. Compounding this was the comparison between her "harmless" transgressions with what to her were such heinous customs as cutting off peoples' hands for stealing and stoning women for adultery. The contrast between the cultures outraged her.

Ed and Andrew aboard transportation, Saudi style

So, she took it out on me by going out without her *abaya* every time she got a chance and deliberately flouting as many other of their rules as she dared. We began to quarrel about what I considered her selfishness and refused to listen when I told her I could be punished for her behavior. Her only answer was that she felt strangled by the smallness of our rooms. Because Andrew was always restless and didn't sleep well, she blamed it on the fact that he had no yard to play in so he could wear off his energy. While I was so tired each night all I wanted to do was rest, she craved getting out and having fun.

Finally it came to the point where we both felt we had had enough. We started making plans for leaving Saudi. But first I had to be sure I had another job to go to. And of course we had to save some money for moving. Valinda again started talking about a job and even of starting a catering business in Riyadh so we could afford to move that much sooner.

In the midst of our planning, the several extensions she had managed to get on her visa ran out. I think in a sense we were both a little relieved. I made up my mind that the next time she got a visa I would have a better place for us to live.

In August I got my holidays and we had another trip back home. Valinda stayed on with her folks for awhile after I left. In September, on her way back to Greece, she stopped off in Toronto to see my folks.

Valinda liked Toronto. She also liked Dad's swimming pool and his wine. My sister had just lost her husband and needed cheering up so while Dad and Mother played Grandpa and Grandma, Valinda and Sis went out on the town. They went shopping a the Yorkdale boutiques, saw a play at the O'Keefe Centre and made a trip to the CNE. It was the Agriculture Building at the CNE which fascinated Valinda the most.

There is a sign as you drive into Valinda's hometown which reads "Beiseker, the Wheat King Capital of the World." Those wheat kings farmed on land Valinda knew and it was at the Toronto winter fairs that they had won their titles. "Beiseker may not have much," Valinda would say, "but it grows the best wheat in the world. Put that in your encyclopedias and smoke it."

Eventually I shared Valinda's allegiance to wheat. One fall Harvey took me out to a field he was preparing to harvest. Through his eyes he made me see, not just the beauty but the satisfaction of looking over a quarter-mile stretch of golden grain that he and his sons had raised on sod first turned by his father.

"How do you know when it's ready to harvest?" I asked.

"I rub a few kernels in my hand and chew them. The harder they are, the better the grade."

There was something to a life where between what you planted and what you ate was only a slim stalk you raised yourself.

My folks were dyed-in-the-wool Easterners. "What is so different about the West?" they would ask Valinda. She was invariably as expansive as every Westerner gets when they try to describe "God's country." Even as I'd watch she seemed to don a baseball cap and start chewing on a straw. Once she wrote her feelings down for my folks:

When you drive down a country road you can see the prairie dogs standing on their hind legs on the edge of the gravel with such a cheeky look, they seem to be saying 'Howdy.' Along the fences tumbleweeds pile up and in a bad year soil from the fields forms in drifts behind the tumbleweeds. In winter you hope enough snow will fall on the fields so there will be snowdrifts along the fences and a moist seed-bed in the spring. The best day of the year is when you hear the honking of the first geese coming north. The caw of the first crow sends the farmer to his machine shed to get the tractor ready for spring work. The worst sight in summer is when it forgets to rain and the sloughs dry up with an ever-widening white rim of alkali around them.

"Everything stops, even the odd curling game, during calving time. Farmers have to be ready night and day to help a cow in difficulty. The loss of a calf can mean hundreds of dollars, perhaps thousands if it's an exotic breed. On the horse ranches they wait just as anxiously for the foals to drop.

If you love trees the prairies are not for you. Grandma Gilberg used to say even prayer couldn't make a tree grow in Alberta. Chinooks kill them. Every time a chinook comes the tree thinks it's spring and the sap starts to move up. Of course most Albertans can't wait for the chinook arch to appear and the warm wind to move, like God's hand, across the land but for tree lovers it is the kiss of death. They resign themselves once more to a shrub where their tree was supposed to be. Actually if you do manage to grow an honest-to-God tree in Alberta it is usually a cottonwood and they get a mixed reception. The female cottonwoods shed so much 'white wool' that most macho Western males would rather cut them down than clean up after them.

The West is like chocolates or crackers and dip. Once you've had a taste you have to go back for more.

Valinda's last visa came in November.

There was a direct flight to Riyadh, as I told her in my final letter before she was to leave Greece. But Valinda, still determined to build up our savings as fast as she could, figured she could save several hundred dollars by going via Cairo to Dhahran. I warned her it would mean a four-hour drive for me from Riyadh to Dhahran as well as a tedious stopover for her in Cairo. I was so concerned I phoned and begged her to take the easier route, reminding her that with all the luggage she always carried it would be a very hard trip. She insisted she could stand all the aggravation and trouble. She was a determined woman when she set her mind to something.

I left Riyadh in the afternoon of November 23 and stayed overnight near Dhahran with a Lebanese couple. Valinda knew them too and because they also had a new child, we planned to spend a few days with them on the way back.

On the morning of November 24, I said a see-you-soon goodbye to my friends and drove to Dhahran airport to meet my family.

I was still waiting for them.

It got warmer in the airport as the day wore on and I was beginning to wish I had stayed in my air-conditioned hotel room longer. However, the wait finally ended; a plane's arrival was announced. It was from Cairo so it must be the one Valinda had caught.

I saw the plane land and then watched with growing anticipation as people started to get off. Once more I was reminded of how often I had done this in the past two years. Valinda and I had become so accustomed to taking planes it was like catching buses at home.

I was still quite relaxed except that I was bored with waiting. I certainly had no sensation of worry as I waited to see them coming off the plane. Valinda would muddle through as she always did. Still, I wished she wouldn't court disaster as she often seemed to. She was sometimes careless. Like this trip. When I phoned she admitted she hadn't reconfirmed her flight. I warned her she could be bumped. She had laughed and assured me it hadn't happened before and wouldn't now. Then there was the stopover in Cairo. What if she had overslept? She had a habit of doing that, especially if Andrew was restless at the beginning of her sleep.

There were a dozen ways she could screw up. Now, watching the passengers get off and not seeing her among them, I began to wonder if she had done it again. At first I was more annoyed than concerned. But as I saw the last of the passengers leave and finally the crew get off with still no sight of her, my annoyance turned to worry.

Searching now, somewhat fearfully, for an explanation as to why I had not seen her among the disembarking passengers, I told myself that I had simply missed her and she was down collecting her luggage. I knew how thorough the checks were on incoming flights, mainly because the Saudi authorities always looked so assiduously for pornographic material and liquor, so I consoled myself with the thought that this was the reason she had not yet appeared. There were always line-ups and delays and with all the luggage she carried, Valinda would hold up the line more than anyone else.

Hours later, or so it seemed, the whole area was cleared and I was still there, with no Valinda or Andrew in sight. I sat, head in hands, wondering what to do. If she had missed the plane she might be stuck in Cairo for 24 hours. If she'd been bumped in Athens, had she already grabbed a later plane? If she had been stuck in either of these places wouldn't she be trying to get in touch with me? Perhaps she was. Perhaps she had already got in touch with my friends in Dhahran. I berated myself for wasting so much time at the airport when I might already have been preparing to meet them at another time. Full of new hope, I phoned my friends.

They had not heard from her.

My new found hope slipped away into fear and anxiety again. If only Valinda had been more predictable I mightn't have been in this mess. If only she wasn't so headstrong and impulsive I wouldn't be having all this worry

My anxiety was rapidly turning to anger.

I felt so helpless. In a case like this where did you turn? In this part of the country where the man made the decisions they'd be inclined to laugh at me if I admitted I wasn't sure what plane my wife was going to be on. Exasperated at myself and at Valinda, I made my way to the Egypt Air office. They must know something. I knew it was a frail hope but I had to grasp at it. Still, I wasn't too surprised when they disclaimed any information about the plane. What did surprise me was the sharpness in the way they answered me. There seemed no reason for it. I stood there staring helplessly, hopelessly at them. Most of the clerks standing around looked away from me.

I didn't know whether they couldn't, or wouldn't, look me in the face.

I continued to stand there. I didn't know what else to do.

And then one chap motioned me over to his desk. At first I thought the look in his eyes was of pain but I was soon to learn it was compassion. The words he said to me were shattering.

"The plane you asked about has been hijacked. It is now in Malta. It is believed that an Egyptian Commando Unit has just assaulted the plane in an attempt to rescue the passengers."

I staggered out of the airport.

Chapter 4

Assault

The assault on the plane came the evening of the second day. During the almost 24 hours preceding it, the terror had been building inevitably to this moment. I could feel it in the wireless clutched in my stiff hand, in my body aching with cold. Terror and anguish. Yes, anguish. We could still feel anguish in my part of the world.

I, Abram Goldman, had seen a second Israeli woman dragged out by the hair to be shot. By now there must be three bodies under the plane. Were they all mingling their blood with the soil of Malta? The third to be shot that night had been a young man, according to the wireless an American. The wireless said there were ten Americans on board. It would be a long night of killing. I shuddered.

In fact, there was only one more that night and it was a woman, "an American woman," added the voice over the wireless. I accepted that additional information almost casually. Were we growing so accustomed to killing that who was killed was only an afterthought? If we, who watched, were that detached, what about those who killed? What about the hijackers? Having killed four was there any incentive for them to stop?

Once during the night there had been the reassuring sight of an Air Malta van delivering food to the plane. I was thankful to think of the comfort food and a hot drink would bring to those besieged passengers. About the same time I even managed a coffee and a doughnut for myself. After the food came the plane seemed to grow strangely still – almost remote. As if it wasn't part of this world. It looked so innocent sitting there hiding all the violence within its walls. I wondered if even hijackers needed to replenish their will to kill. Or were they just trying to decide what to do next since the 15-minute killings hadn't brought them any fuel?

From the wireless I had learned that the Maltese were trying almost continually to negotiate with the hijackers. While still firmly refusing to give them fuel until all the passengers were safe, they were also almost certainly repeating their suggestion that the hijackers' best way out of the impasse was to surrender. They would surely also have reminded them that at least in Malta their lives would be secure. The Prime Minister himself tried to reason with them. He reiterated the plea that they surrender.

The night rain dripped on. I could imagine the passengers gazing dully at the plane windows mesmerizing themselves with the sight of the raindrops sliding down the glass in rivulets. Willing themselves to forget the horror around them. Willing their thoughts to flee to happier times. Gilda and I liked to make love on rainy nights. The patter of the rain on the roof had a sensual sound, a sort of foreplay accompaniment to our own touching and stroking. I hoped some of the people on that plane were able, by means of the rain, to flee to the arms of lovers.

I tried to picture the interior of the plane during these hours when every passenger, every crew member, every hijacker must know that their lives hung in the balance. They were like tightrope walkers with no net. In a sense the crew were in the best spot. They knew the hijackers needed them enough to keep them alive. The hijackers were actually the most vulnerable. Their only out was to win their demands or face death or imprisonment. The passengers, if one was to judge by former hijackings, had the best odds. Their very number made it likely that most of them would survive.

But if I were sitting on that plane would I be thinking rationally? What would I be thinking? Where would my thoughts be? Would their lives pass before their eyes, as was said to happen during extreme danger? Would they be remembering their mother's breast, their father's work-hardened hands, their first day at school, their first kiss, their first act of sex, their first job, their wedding day, their divorce, their retirement, their homeland? If they were Jews or Arabs their homeland was probably what they would be remembering.

Were any of them wondering who would be next after the Americans were all killed? How must it feel knowing that your life depended on your nationality? Caucasians of course were the most vulnerable. Englishmen, Australians, Canadians. Canadians were often confused with Americans. I wouldn't want to be a Canadian on that plane.

An Air Malta van again approached the plane. More food. Killing was a hungry business. I watched white-coated men deliver boxes of food to the flight platform. The plane door opened and the food disappeared. I wondered how many passengers were still able to eat.

Before leaving, the white-coated figures went under the plane and reappeared carrying what I assumed was the last body. What had happened to the others? Had they all died instantly or had the others managed to escape under cover of darkness? It was a bit of hope to cling to.

Time dragged on. It was getting dark again. It would soon be 24 hours since the plane had landed on this Saturday night. For some of those people, Saturday night was probably the fun night of the week. The night people went out and had a party.

I could not keep from thinking about those people, wondering about them. Had they tried to get messages to their loved ones, scratching what could be their last words surreptitiously on the back of a seat, tracing them on the inside grime of a window pane, writing them on a vomit bag? Had businessmen scrawled wills disposing of their property? In their thoughts, had husbands told wives they loved them, had wives emotionally set their husbands free to complete their lives? Had grandparents simply said goodbye to each other and to their loved ones?

I knew I was letting my writer's emotions carry me away. Perhaps it was because I was lightheaded from exhaustion. A moment later I was sure it was neither lightheadedness nor writer's instinct which alerted me to the certainty that in the deepening darkness something was happening. The moment I had been subconsciously awaiting was upon us.

I realized that, encouraged by periods of apparent inactivity on the plane, I had allowed myself to hope that the end might be different than I feared. Now I knew it wasn't going to be.

Suddenly the night air was split by an explosion. No, three explosions. The bursts of smoke and light came from beneath the plane, at the back and front and in the middle. An exit door was flung open. A man tumbled out. At the same time other men seemed to be rushing into the plane. Over it all was the keening of women and the smell of burning flesh.

The end had come for all of us in different ways; for the passengers on the plane, for those of us keeping vigil on the ground, even for the hijackers.

Except for bashed-in exit doors and the smoke smearing its once shiny sides, the plane looked little different than before. Except that now it entombed the dead. And they must be dead. They couldn't have lived through those explosions and the gunfire that followed.

For the first time since all this began, I suddenly felt a sense of hurt so real it seemed almost as though it must bleed through my pores. I had begun this vigil for my fellow countrymen but now felt akin to all those on the plane. They were all my people. Emotionally they belonged to me as much as to all those relatives who would now soon be told the shattering news.

Their loved ones were dead.

Chapter 5

Ordeal

My first instinct as a husband and father was to get to Malta but even as distraught as I was, I knew that such a move didn't make sense. For one thing, with a hijacking in progress or just having ended, no planes would be allowed to land. On top of that, I knew only too well that you had to have an exit visa to leave Saudi and that could take as long as a week.

I got on the phone. My only hope was to get a visa pushed through sooner, if I could get the right people working on it. Surely I had good grounds.

I called the Canadian Embassy. During the long day I called again and again, my anger rising. Someone must be on duty, even on Sunday. What if there were a world crisis? Did our embassy only take notice of events that happened during the week? They had to know about the hijacking. Wouldn't they have been notified if there were Canadians on board?

"If" there were? I still had this fugitive hope that Valinda and Andrew were safe on some other plane. But the hope was growing weaker.

When I couldn't get through to the Embassy, I decided to see if anything could be done from Canada. Dad had a long-time friend, Senator Stanley Haidaz, who might have some clout. It was the first time I had tried to contact my folks since the airport clerk had told me the news, mostly because I wanted to be sure Valinda was on the plane before I alerted them. Had I been thinking straight I would have realized that the authorities would have notified my parents and the Uffelmans, especially since I couldn't be reached. I hadn't left my Lebanese friends' address with anyone. After all, we had expected this to be as routine as Valinda's other trips.

Dad's first words shattered my composure. "We're so sorry, Ed."

"I know, Dad. Have you been in touch with Valinda's folks? I don't think I can talk to them yet."

"We've been talking to them. They're holding up – still hoping."

"Where are you, Ed?" my mother asked.

"Stuck here in Dhahran. Of course I'm trying to get to Malta. I thought the Canadian Embassy would help me but they aren't even answering the phone. You'd think someone would have told them!" The anger that had been building up all day was not far from the surface.

"What can we do, Ed?"

"I was wondering about the Senator. Do you think he could do something?" Stanley Haidaz had been our family doctor and he and my father shared a common heritage.

"I'll call him as soon as I hang up," Dad promised.

"Keep in touch, son," my mother said. "We're thinking of you every moment."

"Thanks, Mom. Bye," I mumbled and got off the phone.

Senator Haidaz must have swung into action right away. In a surprisingly short time I got a call from the Canadian ambassador in Riyadh, who said they were putting a man full-time on my case. The first thing they would do was get me an exit visa, they promised. In the meantime they advised me to go back to my apartment in Riyadh until they called. I went back to Riyadh but to my office, not the apartment. I wasn't sure I could face it yet.

There was no one in the office as I went in. I was thankful. I still wasn't ready to talk. But there was some comfort in the office itself and in the familiarity of my desk and chair. Of course I didn't try to work. I couldn't even remember what I had been doing when I left to meet Valinda. I sat, staring at the wall, staring at my desk. Eventually my general manager came in. After expressing his sympathy, he offered to phone Malta for me. He got through with surprising ease although all my attempts had failed.

He confirmed that Valinda and Andrew were on the plane. My hope was shredded because his information was so exact. He even got their middle names. I knew those names could only have come from their passports.

The Canadian Embassy called. "There has been a report that all the children are dead," the man on the phone said carefully. "We are not sure about your wife. There are some badly injured people who haven't been identified."

"Badly injured? Do you mean wounded, blown apart by a grenade, burned?" I flung the words at him.

"I can't say, Mr. Leonard. We don't know any more."

"Why don't you?" I rasped. "And why am I sitting here? I should be in Malta with my wife in case she needs me."

"I know," said the man soothingly. "As I told you we're working on your visa."

Although at that moment I may have had my doubts as to their sincerity, I was thankfully surprised at how soon they managed to get me a visa. But my problems weren't over yet. There wasn't a plane until late that night. I was in for another interminable 12-hour wait.

I went back to our apartment and my friends began to arrive. They each brought a bottle of the liquor every Westerner in Saudi hoards and keeps hidden for just such an emergency. I supposed what we were doing was holding a wake for Valinda, only there was no body. And the people sharing it with me were trying to convince me there would be no body.

I knew different. I tried to make plans for not coming back because I knew I never would if Valinda and Andrew were gone. I had been growing a moustache, mostly to see the look on Valinda's face when she saw it. I went in the bathroom and shaved it off. There would be no laughter in her happy face for me anymore.

I began sorting through our belongings, throwing out or giving my friends what I didn't want to keep. Packing the things I wanted. I wasn't doing a very good job of it. The hardest part was the toys Andrew had left and a bathing suit of Valinda's.

"She wore it the first time she swam in the Red Sea," I mumbled. I could still see her feet as she stood there, wide-footed in the sand and said, "I wonder if Moses stood here?" She had odd feet, flat with a wide space between her big toe and the next one. I clung to the suit for a moment and then said to one of my co-workers, "Do you want to give this to your wife?"

"You don't have to do this," he said. "Leave things as they are, you'll be back. And if you're not . . . well it will be time to think about it then. We'll take care of things until you know one way or the other."

I had drunk too much to really care. I gave up on the packing.

About 2 a.m. the representative from the Canadian Embassy who had been assigned to travel with me, picked me up. It was to be a long, hard, 14-hour trip before we reached Malta. In my state of exhaustion and with the liquor I had drunk, I was hardly conscious of it. I remember stopping at Zurich and then a stopover at Rome. The latter was to become impressed on my memory when five weeks later another hijacking took place not far from where we sat awaiting our plane.

We arrived in Malta shortly after noon. I hadn't slept for 48 hours. A peculiar odor hung over the airport. I realized what it was when they drove me to one of the airport hangars, where the Maltese had set up a makeshift morgue. Under the blazing sun the sickly sweet scent reminded me of Valinda's sensitivity to smell. How she had hated the smell of the cattle feed lot on the farm in Beiseker and the stench of the camels in Cairo. She would have hated this smell too.

We had to wait outside the morgue. The guards didn't want too many people in there at one time.

"There are some Egyptian families in there now," someone said needlessly. We could hear them crying and wailing and there was the occasional shriek of horrified recognition.

"I'm not going to be able to go through this," I thought. I felt sick and walked away from the building to get a breath of clean air.

The next ones allowed in were the Greek families and from what we could hear they seemed to be almost mad with grief. I covered my ears to shut out the sounds of their screaming and moaning. Even muffled, there was an angry undercurrent to the sounds and although I couldn't understand what they were saying I knew it must be what I was thinking: if I could only get my hands on the hijackers, the people who had caused it. The people who had turned our relatives, our loved ones into those foul-smelling rows of bodies.

I was glad Andrew wasn't there. As the only fair-haired boy aboard the flight, he had been positively identified and taken to the University morgue. But Valinda, the wholesome, laughing girl I had loved, was in this horrible place. Once the Greeks had grown a little quieter, the guard let me in. The medical examiner looked up at me as I paused before his table and gave him my name. He said he hadn't been able to positively identify a Canadian lady. Oh God, was there still hope?

The bodies were laid out in two rows. It was horrible, worse than I had feared. None of the bodies had been cleaned. Some were disembowelled, some were burned, some were mutilated. After I'd gone past the first row, I was staggering. I turned unsteadily toward the other side of the room and there was Valinda. I recognized her by the bottoms of her feet. Those flat soles, the wide space between the two first toes. I remembered how the sand along the Red Sea had come up between her toes.

She wasn't mutilated or hurt in any way as far as I could see. If some one had only taken the trouble to wash her it would be just as though she were resting. Suddenly the Greeks surged forward and I feared they would trample her as they found one of their own beside her. I wanted to throw myself over her to save her from them. But I didn't. I signed the forms identifying her and left.

I still hadn't seen Andrew. I got a taxi to take me to the University and the morgue. Before asking to see him I found a washroom and splashed water on my face. The water cooled my hot forehead. The serenity of the antiseptically white walls and basins and the non-glare lighting had a soothing effect. My Dad, as a builder, had always said, "Don't neglect the bathrooms. More marriages have been saved by a good-sized bathroom than by a psychiatrist. It's the perfect place to cool off and calm down."

There was a lot in that. In the lifetime of the average person, condemned to the cramped quarters of assembly lines, the narrow cubicles of offices, the confines of commuting vehicles, even the shopping aisles of stores, the most space each individual would ever have to themselves was a good-sized bathroom. I knew what he was getting at as the peace and quiet of this empty and echoless room flowed through me. I also knew I was thinking of things like that so I wouldn't have to think of Andrew. When I finally left the seclusion of the bathroom and walked out into the hall I was ready for what was ahead of me.

Andrew looked as though he were sleeping. I touched his little hand but the fingers no longer curled around mine in perfect confidence as they had in the past. Now it was my fingers curling around his tiny ones and clinging desperately to him.

"I saw Mommy," I said brokenly. "She's . . ." and then I realized that if my belief was as strong as Leah's, I wouldn't be saying this. I would know that Andrew and Valinda were already together.

"I wish I were with you," I mumbled, not quite sure what I meant. I couldn't pull my gaze away from the small white face and the golden hair. "Kiki will miss you. Grandpa Leonard thought you'd be a builder. Grandpa Uffelman said you'd be a farmer. Of course your mother was sure you'd be a doctor or a lawyer or the prime minister of Canada. We had such dreams and hopes for you. Instead you were just a baby. How we loved you, Andrew. How so many people loved you."

The Embassy official got me a room in a Malta hotel and again I tried to sleep. Perhaps I did for awhile but at the same time I seemed part of a wide-awake nightmare. When I finally gave up and got out of bed, something drew me back to the airport. Maybe I felt closer to Valinda there, maybe I was looking for something; an explanation, a reason for all this happening.

Almost without realizing how it happened, I found myself talking to a reporter. He was Jewish and had haunted eyes. I didn't realize until after that what was haunting him was what he had just seen. All I could tell was that he looked as bereft as I felt and that he acted as though he knew me. He told me his name was Abram Goldman.

"I've been here since this all began," he said in a tired voice. "I saw them throw the bodies out, I saw the plane explode. Later I saw them dragging out – I mean carrying out – the bodies and taking them over there." He motioned to the building where I had found Valinda.

"You found her," he said. "I knew there would be women on board who would leave men like you. It was sometimes as though I could see through those plane walls to where the people waited to die, your wife, your little boy." He beckoned me to follow him. "Here is where they brought the belongings. There was a child's pushcart. They said the Egyptians had to remove it from the cargo hold before they could go in. We can't go inside here but I thought you'd want to know about it. It's about the only thing that didn't die on that plane."

I looked at him, pondering his strange use of words. "How do you know so much about all this when you were outside just like we are now?"

"I have interviewed the pilot, Captain Galal and some of the passengers."

"Did the pilot ever say why they did it, what they wanted?"

He shook his head. "Not really."

"Did he say anything about the hijackers?"

"Again not much. He did say the hijacker who is alleged to have done the killings never tried to justify anything. He was very calm after each shooting and on at least three occasions, whistled and sometimes even hummed. The last time the pilot saw the hijacker whom he believes did the killing, he was walking down the aircraft aisle with a grenade in his hand."

I turned my face away from the reporter, unable to listen to more. In my mind's eye I could see that hijacker making his way down the plane, preparing to throw his grenade. And I asked myself in agony what Valinda must be thinking as she watched him come toward her. No, I thought she probably wouldn't have seen him because she would have thrown her body over Andrew's to protect him. At least if her head were down she would have been spared the look in that madman's eyes.

"He's alive you know," the reporter said. "In St. Luke's Hospital with the victims.

"Oh God, no. Valinda's in that building, that morgue, on a cement floor and he's in a comfortable hospital bed being cared for."

In the trauma of the past few days I had thought very little of the hijackers, individually or personally. They had been lumped together as "the enemy;" the terrible unknown force doing uncontrollable things to my family and others. Now, as I listened to the reporter, they began to take shape in my mind.

Two of them had died, I now knew. One of them, I had been told, died in the same area and I supposed in the same way as Valinda. The real horror of the thought hit me. One of those men, the one who had done all the shooting according to the pilot, was in a hospital room only yards from where I was.

I excused myself and went back to my hotel room. While I might walk away from the reporter, I couldn't walk away from my thoughts. I could not stop thinking of the hijacker in that hospital. I knew if I left Malta without an attempt to see him I would never be able to rest.

Another thought had begun to grow in my mind. The survivors were undoubtedly at St. Luke's, as well. Maybe some of them would talk with me. Maybe some of them would remember Valinda and Andrew. Maybe they could tell me how she died.

Embassy officials were making arrangements by phone and telegraph to fly my family and me home to Canada, which made it all seem remote. I began to feel I had little to do with it all, other than being the reason for it. I realized I would have nothing to do while the interminable government red tape was processed. Why not go to the hospital?

I had a bit of luck soon after I arrived at St. Luke's. I was at the desk, trying to make the receptionist understand that I wanted to speak to someone who had been on the plane. She obviously thought I was a reporter hunting for a story so was giving me the run-around. Someone tapped me on the shoulder.

"I'm Tony Lyons," said an Australian voice. "I was on that plane. And right now I'm bored as hell. Maybe I can help you. How about a cuppa?"

Tony was an outgoing chap, I soon discovered and he seemed to want to talk. "What's your name?" he asked. "And who did you have onboard?"

"My wife Valinda and my little boy Andrew," I answered.

"Ay? His mother had dark hair?" he asked. I nodded, almost afraid to believe my luck.

"I remember them," he said, "and I'll tell you why. There was another Aussie on that plane and she was sitting with your wife for awhile. I was right behind them – until they started rearranging us and moved me to the front. Ready for the slaughter, I reckoned. Who do you kill after Israelis and Americans? Aussies or Canadians?"

"She was quite calm most of the time," Tony went on. "The only time she got a little rattled was when the oxygen masks dropped down. She put Andrew's on first and that almost got her into trouble."

"She knew better," I mumbled.

"They always tell Mothers to put their own on first. I suppose it's one of those things that sounds good in theory but when you have to do it. Mothers are too accustomed to putting their children first."

"But she did get his on – and hers too?" I don't know why I cared because it hadn't been able to help them.

"Oh yes. Funny thing, it was the only time I saw one of the hijackers act human. The one at the back was trying to help her. He really seemed worried about your little boy."

I swallowed hard. I couldn't talk about Andrew now.

"You saw the hijackers? All of them?"

"Yes. But you know they had masks on. Still there were things you noticed – about the way they moved and spoke and the look of their eyes even behind their masks. The one that did the killing, he had such hard, cold eyes. He seemed to enjoy what he was doing."

"How could you see his eyes from the back of the plane?"

"I couldn't. But I had been sitting close to him before the hijacking began. I got a good look at him before they moved me to the back along with the Aussie girl and your wife and son."

"Valinda must have been at the front at first if she was moved to the back when you were. She must have seen his eyes too."

"Yes, I'm sure she got a good look at him but at that time he did not seem to be so dangerous. It was only later. I doubt if your wife quite realized what danger she was in, sitting at the back away from the shooting. You have that to be thankful for. And if it's any comfort to you, I think she died suddenly."

"It is a comfort just talking to you," I said, "You'll never know how much. Especially because you saw them."

After a moment, Tony glanced sideways at me. "The hijacker's here, you know. He's on the floor above. I can take you to the ward but they won't let you in."

They didn't. As I gazed at the closed door behind which a hijacker lay, I vowed I'd spend the rest of my life trying to save others from suffering the pain this terrorist had caused me. In my own small way, in that moment I declared war on terrorism.

The Canadian Embassy representative had the arrangements all made when I got back to the hotel. The next morning Valinda and Andrew boarded their last plane, homeward-bound, Beiseker-bound.

Chapter 6

Goodbye

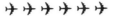

The night Ed flew back from Malta with my daughter's body I had to be alone. I slipped away after Harvey and the family had left to meet the plane and walked, at first aimlessly, around the yard. It was after dark but the snow made it light enough to see. There was a certain comfort in its familiar crunch under my feet.

I passed the feed lot and heard the cattle snuffling as they chewed their cud and rested. I touched a tree in the yard I used to share with Grandma Uffelman. I had planted it for Valinda's first birthday. It would go on living and reaching for the sky, but Valinda . . .

"Oh Valinda, Valinda," I sobbed. I ran on until I found myself at the edge of a field where I sank down in the furrow that separated it from the trees. Wrapping myself in my heavy coat, I rocked back and forth and let the grief pour out of me.

I remembered Valinda's ninth birthday when she and her friends had sat in this furrow and tried to smoke. Of course I knew they were there and what they were doing. I had seen them disappearing around the corner with guilty looks on their faces, the odor of banana peels trailing them and the toilet paper half hidden under their coats. But I saw no harm in it. I was glad they had a way of amusing themselves – there was no nicotine in banana peels.

Those weren't the only memories assailing me that night. There was the little house in Beiseker where she had been conceived. There were the months as I waited impatiently for her to be born. During the last month, in order to make it go faster, I went with Harvey each morning to the farm.

My happiest moments were every afternoon when he would drive out to the fields to test the readiness of the grain for combining. I'd sit in the truck cab, mesmerized by the sun glinting off the hood and feeling warm and cosseted by its rays as they shone through the open window on my face and shoulders. I could hear the light breeze stirring the grass and the slap of brittle grain heads against overalls as Harvey walked through the fields, stopping now and again to pick a stalk, rub it in his hands, blow away the chaff and then chew the meaty kernels between his strong white teeth.

If he took time to test several spots in the field I would doze in the sun until the child-in-a-hurry inside of me would give a vigorous kick and startle me awake. I had the vague feeling that this unborn child already resented being hemmed in, even by her mother's womb. I would sit and daydream about the coming baby. I suspected Harvey, like most men, was hoping for a boy. I didn't care. All I wanted was this baby in my arms. Harvey's baby.

I was standing watching Harvey and his father working on the machinery in preparation for starting the harvest next day when my water broke. My feet were in the soil of this very furrow. There had been something symbolic about the water surrounding Valinda mixing with this soil. I wondered if she ever felt the emotional pull of the Alberta soil as I did.

We were surprisingly relaxed for a young couple having their first baby. From the field, we went back to Beiseker, got washed up and then drove the 40 miles to the hospital in Calgary.

The real pains started about 10 p.m. I wanted Harvey to stay with me but in those days husbands were not allowed in labor rooms. However the nurse finally agreed to let him sit with me because he had so far to drive back home. He was still with me when the baby finally arrived at 5 a.m., August 21st.

The first thing I noticed about her was her toes. They were exactly like Harvey's, with a wide space between the first and second toes. Valinda was a beautiful, healthy baby weighing 7 lbs. 14 ozs and measuring 21 inches. I couldn't stop gazing at her in wonderment.

Some ten days after she was born, we brought her home. The weather had turned, as it so often does in harvest time and had been raining for some days. We had to slosh through mud with our pink-shawled little darling. Harvey didn't seem to feel as disgruntled as he usually did about a harvest rain because it gave him time to hold the baby.

He couldn't get over how tiny and fragile this new life was. He had spent his life around "big" things – cattle, horses, machinery. It didn't seem possible this little bundle could ever grow into an adult. One day he put her in a shoebox and set her on top of the fridge. We laughed uproariously. She was so cute and looked so ridiculous. A baby in a shoebox on top of a fridge. Like a radiator cap on a car.

That fall we bought a small house and moved it out beside the Uffelman's homesite. For the first few weeks our house had no foundation, no plumbing and no furnace because Harvey was too busy harvesting to work on it. It was often cold and uncomfortable. I could keep the baby warm while she was sleeping but when I had to change or bathe her, she shuddered at the cold blast of air. It was Valinda's first reminder that the world was not always going to be as warm and comforting as her mother's womb.

She was a healthy child. In fact she was so naturally healthy that she took it as a real affront if she ever took sick. We had a hard time hiding our amusement when, at about four years, she had her first stomach upset. After going through the indignity of bringing up over the toilet bowl, she looked coldly at us and said, "I'm not enjoying this one bit, you know."

She was two years old when Vance was born. Like most children accustomed to the limelight, she didn't take kindly to this intrusion into her territory. However she had her Grandma Uffelman to fill the gap. When I was busy with the new baby she would run over to Grandma to be cuddled.

"My little Madja," Grandma Uffelman would call her. Sometimes she'd rock her to sleep telling her stories of the old country and how they came to Canada.

"We got off the train," she'd begin. "We were so tired and hungry. There were people all around us speaking a language we couldn't understand. We didn't know where to go, which door to go out of once Grandpa managed to get all our luggage off the train and piled around us. We just stood there wondering what to do next.

Suddenly we heard a voice we could understand and a woman in a *baboushka* came over to us. She was from our hometown in Russia and had recognized your grandfather. They had left Russia about the same time as we had gone to Buenos Aires. Her family had come to Canada. She took us home with her that night and the next day helped us find a place to live. We began to love this new country that day."

Probably from spending so much time with her grandparents, Valinda was old for her age. My family called her "the little old lady." She never talked baby talk. Harvey and I were so delighted at her ability to talk well at an early age that we devised a set of questions to ask her and then would preen ourselves when the family exclaimed at what a clever child she was. When we asked "Who is the premier of Alberta?" she'd answer "Manning." When we asked who was the prime minister of Canada, she'd say "Pearson." When we asked who the president of the United States was and she triumphantly sang out, "John Fitzgerald Kennedy," she brought the house down. Of course no one was unkind enough to mention that we always asked the questions in the same order so her rote answers could be compared to counting to 100.

She was a pretty little girl, rosy-cheeked, blue-eyed and with naturally curly hair. Because she was so pretty, I loved to buy her clothes. I can still see her in the first school outfit I bought her. Mother and I went shopping together at the Bay. Mother was buying an outfit for Tanya, the granddaughter she was raising after my sister Mona died. The difference was that Mother was just buying clothes that day and I was shopping for something special for my special little daughter. I bought her a red blazer with gold buttons. I was so proud of that outfit.

Valinda's first teacher was Mrs. Verhaest. I handed over my little doll in her red blazer, my eyes full of tears. Mrs. Verhaest assured me she had seen countless mothers and first children through this traumatic experience and they had all survived!

Valinda and Shelly and Cathy all started school together. I was afraid she wouldn't get along with the other kids as she hadn't been around many children her own age. I worried at first that she might be a "loner." I sometimes sat outside the school at afternoon recess to watch her in the schoolyard. Often she seemed to be walking around by herself. I used to wonder what she was thinking in those solitary moments and wish she were laughing and playing with the others.

One afternoon while I was sitting watching, Mrs. Verhaest came to talk to me about Valinda's progress and expressed surprise at the grasp she had of language.

"She would never use a word like 'ain't'," she said laughingly. "In fact she corrects the others when they do. But it is the abstract words that surprise me. Today I asked the class to describe the schoolyard after everyone was gone. Most of them said what I expected, 'empty.' Valinda said, 'abandoned.' Now where would a child of six get a word like that?" she marvelled.

"Abandoned." I shuddered. Had that been the word in Valinda's mind as she sat on the plane and eventually was abandoned even by hope?

There was no window in Valinda's bedroom when she was growing up. She did not seem to need one. It was as though she could see things we couldn't. My mother used to say she saw the flower garden while we were still planting the seeds. I had to believe, it was part of my Christian faith, that she had gone, as my mother called it, to a "better place." I had to believe for my own peace of mind, that in those last few moments before she died, she had seen flowers in her life's garden.

I shivered. I was cold. There were tears frozen on my cheeks. But before I said my final goodbye there was one thing yet I had to do.

I went back to the house and to the room where we kept the possessions even Valinda hadn't been able to drag around. Rummaging about, I found the box that Valinda had laughingly told me on her last visit was her legacy to me.

"My Uffel-mush, Mom, it's all yours," she had teased. "I know you've always wanted to read it."

In a way she was right. I had often thought if I could read it, I would understand her better. Valinda didn't keep a diary but anything she took the time to write, she treasured. It always ended up in her "Uffel-mush." I never knew what Uffel-mush stood for but it seemed to mean anything that concerned her and her family.

Sometimes she wrote bits about our family history for class assignments; other times, she spent rainy days writing about her friends and relatives, about our car, the animals, whatever interested her and her interests were varied.

Hard as it might be, I knew I could never let go of Valinda until I had faced her Uffel-mush box. Actually the box was not as full as I expected it to be. She must have edited it herself over the years. I picked up the first sheet and my eyes blurred at the childish printing. Who is the premier of Alberta? Manning. Who is the president of the United States? John Fitzgerald Kennedy. I choked back the sobs and brushed aside the tears so I could see to read the rest.

I have the blood of many nations in my veins, Valinda had written. In spite of the pain, I had to smile to myself. Even as a child, Valinda thought expansively.

My Uffelman roots go back to Saratov on the banks of the Volga. Their forebears probably came from Germany because they lived in a German-speaking community in Russia. In 1904 they joined a large group of Europeans who were wooed to South America by stories of the good rich soil in Argentina.

My great grandfather George Uffelman and his wife and two sons, one of whom was to become my grandfather, gravitated to a German-speaking community on the edge of the Pampas. The Rio de la Plata river was enough like the Volga that they did not feel too strange.

In 1911 another wave of Russian-born settlers came to the Pampas. Among them was my grandmother-to-be, Elizabeth Michael who married my grandfather Andrew the following year.

In 1913 their first son George was born and died shortly after. My grandmother blamed this hard new country for her baby's death and from that moment on was determined to leave the Pampas, a land so cruelly empty save for its endless miles of grass. She got her way and the family arrived in Calgary, sometime late in 1913.

If her first glimpse of the prairies dismayed my grandmother because of its resemblance to the pampas, she didn't admit to it. But when it came time for them to plant their first wheat crop in Beiseker, the seed came from a little bag of grain she had secreted among their belongings. She did not have to tell my grandfather that the grain had been hand-reaped from the wheatfield beside which her first born son had had to be left in Argentina.

Grandma Uffelman had nine more children. Her youngest son was my father.

It was the Swedish connection that brought the steel to my mother's family. My grandfather Arvid Gilberg was born in Harbonas, Sweden in 1908. His grandfather had fought in the Napoleonic wars and that was when the family name was changed. It had originally been Maltson but there were so many by that name in Napoleon's army that the paymaster, in desperation, changed some of them. At first the change was to Gilbert but over the years it became Gilberg and that was the name grandfather had when he followed a married brother to Canada and settled in the Irricana area.

About the only thing, aside from his healthy body, that Grandfather Gilberg brought to Canada was a stern admonition from his father that "if you don't work, you don't eat." Paradoxically, his father who was a magistrate in his Swedish homeland was on a committee that eventually produced the world's first old age pension. Probably the first people of the working class ever to receive something for nothing!

When Grandpa Gilberg met my grandmother she was still driving 32 miles each Sunday, to church and back. She and her family made the trip in a horse and buggy in summer and a team and sled in winter. She endured those hours of burning heat and biting blizzards because of her father's devotion to the church. Grandpa promised her the first thing he'd buy her was a car.

Over the years, two things Grandpa loved were cars and auctions – more than once to Grandma's despair. But she still used to say, proudly, that if anyone for miles around wanted a spare part for car or machine, they only had to come to Grandpa.

In 1936 Leah, their fourth daughter was born. She is my mother.

Nearly everyone in Canada has American relations. I did too. My Grandmother Harvine was a McCune. The first McCune came from Ireland to the United States in 1749. The family settled first in Pennsylvania and then in Kansas where there is still a town called McCune named after them. My major ambition is to see it someday.

My great grandfather, Isaac Melville McCune, became a teacher and a lay preacher and a politician. No wonder he was a poor farmer. He preached in the Irricana West Church for 40 years, brought the first piano to the countryside, started the first literary society, sponsored the first chautauqua in the area, and engineered a fence-post telephone system that ended the isolation of many farmers around Irricana.

He turned his wife into the first feminist in the area. Belonging to the Bretheren Church, she was supposed to wear their pre-scribed plain garb and to have no jewellery. Instead, she rebel-liously became the first woman in her husband's congregation to wear modern dress and when he became a member of the legislature she insisted on having a wedding ring. As she logi-cally pointed out how would it look for a mother of four to go to Edmonton without a wedding ring?

I don't know whether my great grandfather was dour or not but the only joke I ever heard of that he cracked concerned his political mentor Aberhart. The family had a picture of Aberhart on the wall and near it there was one of Jesus. When my mother was small she complained that she couldn't tell them apart. Great grandfather McCune said, "Don't worry, Leah. Sometimes Aberhart gets mixed up too."

As I skimmed through the next few sheets I was surprised at how much information Valinda had gathered up about her family. All those times when she was plaguing us with questions, she had been serious about her roots. I felt guilty we had not told her more of our family. However, there had been one time when I had been glad we hadn't given Valinda too many of the family "skeletons."

She was 11 or 12 then and the papers were full of the Biafra famine. Valinda organized a money-making scheme to help them. Of course, being Valinda, it couldn't be something simple like a lemonade stand. Instead she conceived the idea that she and her friends should write their family histories, put them in a book and sell them.

None of the families paid much attention to what they were doing until Valinda and her friends mimeographed the stories and stapled them into books. The excitement started the moment the first book was sold — and obviously read! The phone never stopped ringing. The upshot of it all was that the kids made money all right but for all the wrong reasons. Some families bought all the copies they could lay their hands on and burned them. The rest of us simply paid the girls not to sell anymore copies. No wonder the family was wary of Valinda from then on.

I came to a sheet called "Memories I have." Now the writing had changed from the rounded childish script to a slanted maturity.

When I was five I was ready for school. The school bus went right by our door so one day I hunted up a book and a lunch pail Grandpa Gilberg had got at an auction and I slipped out of the house one morning without Mother hearing me. When I got down the lane I could see the bus coming. I started waving at it to stop. The bus driver was just pulling up when Mother caught me.

"I'd have picked her up," he said. "She seemed to know what she was doing, Leah."

"She always knows what she's doing," Mother said crossly. "But she's got another year to wait."

I could not see for tears. Valinda, Valinda, my impatient girl. Why was she in such a hurry? She ran out of years too soon.

I have taken control of my social life. I put on my own 10th birthday party. I baked my own cake and invited my own guests, Cathy, Shelly, Sheila and Peggy. I decided we were too old for pin the tail on the donkey. It was time we learned to smoke.

I had read that you can smoke dried banana peels. I stored them away with a roll of toilet paper and some matches and when Mother wasn't looking we slipped outside, through the trees beside the house and hid in the back furrow on the edge of the field. We lit up. By the time the toilet paper and matches were gone I was ready to admit that my smoking idea was a flop. So was the whole party.

But in my opinion, my first decade which ended in 1968 hadn't been a flop if only because I had been a part of it. As Cathy would say, I always had a high opinion of myself! In any case other things besides my arrival on the scene had happened in that decade and of course most of them had made more news than I had. Martin Luther King had been assassinated. So had Robert Kennedy. Jackie Kennedy and Aristotle Onassis were getting married. There was a hijacking and the Arabs and Israelis were killing each other. "As usual," Dad always added when that news came on.

In 1968, I, Valinda Uffelman was 10 years old.

In my 14th year I tried beer. We were having a pyjama party at Shelly's. I had read somewhere that the quickest way to get drunk was to drink beer through a straw. Shelly got a bottle of beer out of her father's cabinet and we all sat around, each with a straw stuck in it.

Pretty soon we all began giggling. Partly because we looked so silly and partly because our parents always giggled and laughed when they drank beer. We thought we were drunk just like the grown-ups. We rolled around the floor deliriously happy. I wonder how much it costs to get happy like that when you are older?

I got a Barbie doll for Christmas. It is so tall and slim it makes me sick. Mother and Aunt Inga are slim. They've got small bones. Why did I have to take after the Uffelmans?

I'm wearing glasses now. I hate them. But I have to admit the colors are brighter. And the glasses keep the dust out of my eyes when it is blowing across the fields. Sometimes I think the dust is always blowing in Alberta.

I wonder if glasses will interfere with my kissing. I've had my first date – only it wasn't much like a date. I've known Greg all my life. Still I think he wanted to kiss me. I wonder if I had taken off my glasses if it would have given him a hint?

My grandmother gave me a music box. It plays the theme song from Love Story. I cried when I saw the movie and I still cry every time I play the music box. Ryan O'Neal was such a handsome widower – and so nobly sad. I wanted to rush off and comfort him.

Why is there something more heart-wrenching about a wife dying young and leaving a husband than a husband dying and leaving a young wife? Why do people never forget those who die young? If I died young, would people never forget me?

I'd love to own an encyclopedia. I can read the one at school but I get so little time at it, it's like dip and crackers, I always want more. I want to know everything there is to know. I can't believe that Beiseker isn't even mentioned in it. How can I ever live all my life in a place that isn't even mentioned in the encyclopedia?

I introduced Shelly and Cathy to rum at Camp Hickory United Church Camp. We had to go for an orientation course in April. In order to drink our rum, we had to get away from the councillor so we decided to sleep in a tent in spite of the snow on the ground. We had got our tent up and had our first drink, enough to warm us up and give us the giggles when the tent flap blew open bringing with it a gust of snow. While we were trying to shake off the snow and close the flap the whole tent fell down around us. We were too cold to try to get it up again so we hunted around the building until we found a kitchen window we could open. By then everyone inside was asleep so we crawled in and curled up by the fire.

Shelly and Cathy were sure the councillor would smell the rum in the morning. But the smell of our clothes drying out was so overpowering wo got away with it.

"How do you manage to get out of scrapes so easily?" Shelly said enviously. "You must live a charmed life, Valinda."

One time I wrote an essay on Joey Smallwood. I chose him because Newfoundland was as far away from Alberta as I could get and I also liked the idea of him being a Father of Confederation. I said he was a link with history. Just as I was a blood link between Russia, Germany, Sweden and Ireland. Every man I knew in Alberta wore cowboy boots and cowboy hats, mostly to make them look taller. Joey Smallwood was a small man but he had a tall mind. I think I have a tall mind.

I'm going to get out of Beiseker if it kills me. I've already arranged with my teachers to take extra subjects. If I pass them I'll get out of school six months before the rest of the class. Mother is upset because I'll miss my graduation. She says it's her one chance to see me out of pants.

I'm Calgary bound – pants and all. I'm going to be a nurse's aide. I told the family about it tonight. Vance scoffed at me. "I sure hope I'm never one of your patients," he said. Vance and I have been at loggerheads ever since he ran the wheels off my doll carriage. Vaughn and Verle-Ann were younger so they never bothered me. I could look down on them. "You can have my room," I said, not unkindly, to Verle-Ann.

It is harder to leave home than I had expected. Tonight as I ate supper for the last time with my family I was remembering Grandma and Grandpa Uffelman and Aunt Mary. They had taken a lot of my allotment of love when they went. I missed being Grandma's "little Madja."

I didn't want to leave the table when the others did. I just sat there staring out of the window. I could see the turkey run, the feedlots and beyond them Hagel's Hill where Dad was planning to build our new home. Beyond the hill I could see the road to Acme. Now that it was paved there was no more dust despite the increase in cars whizzing by. I liked to do some of the whizzing – when I could talk Dad out of his car.

I could see in my mind the hundreds of acres of fields surrounding our farmhouse. They were either green with the first seeds pushing through or yellow with heavy heads of grain ripening. The rest of the year they were most often white with snow.

Mother finished clearing the table and I was still sitting there. I looked at the shiny wood after her dishcloth passed over it. In its shiny-worn top I could see reflections of Joey Smallwood, Pierre Elliot Trudeau, Nixon, Hitler, Napoleon, Alexander the Great, Helen of Troy and so many, many others who had peopled my study books.

It isn't really so hard to leave home when you have the key to the universe like this 16-year-old has, I thought complacently as I left Mother and the kitchen to go and pack my suitcase. "Don't you ever leave anything behind?" my mother asked when she saw all that I was taking.

In Calgary I moved in with the Taylor girls from Acme and enrolled in a Registered Nurses Assistant course at the Southern Alberta Institute of Technology. I took my practical training at Foothills Hospital.

I don't know why I chose nursing when I hate taking orders so much. Hospitals have a regular caste system, I soon discovered. They also don't take kindly to new ideas – and I was always full of them. But worst of all they didn't pay much. I wouldn't go back and ask Dad for money so I took a part time job at Tino's Pizza. He was a Greek.

I met Gail in Calgary. She was interested in the occult. When I was in school in Beiseker we had a teacher who told us a strange story about a white horse. It was dancing round and round and as it whirled around it sank deeper and deeper into the sand until it was up to its neck. I could never figure out what it all meant but it seemed to have something to do with the supernatural.

After we heard that story we girls decided to hold a seance. I brought my Ouija board. We all joined hands and waited for something to happen. A cushion fell off the couch. We were sure it was a message. But what message?

Gail introduced me to Tarot cards. I got a deck and kept them with me. Every time Gail told my fortune the death card came up.

The Taylor girls put on a party for my 20th birthday. I had my eye on a new man. I put on a real campaign. I lost weight so I could wear a special dress. I got my hair done, my eyes done, my toenails done. I even went to the dentist and got my teeth cleaned. And then I had a mud pack.

It didn't work. The date flopped. So far as I was concerned the party flopped. My birthday parties seemed to have a habit of doing that.

Before I went to sleep that August 21st night of 1978 I mulled over the second decade of my life. More things seemed to have happened in it than in my first but that was probably because I was now more aware.

The Vietnam war ended, there was the Yom Kippur war and we had a sort of war in Canada. The FLQ were bombing mailboxes and taking hostages. They killed LaPorte and Trudeau invoked military law. Pretty exciting for dull old Canada.

Boys started wearing long hair, girls wore hot pants for a season and then we all ended up in shirts and jeans. There was Watergate and Trudeau married Margaret, a girl my age. Patty Hearst was kidnapped and I had a boy-friend who drove a sin-bin. I never asked him to drive me out to Beiseker. Dad would have flipped.

My favorite TV program was Happy Days and if I wasn't in love that particular week I dreamed about the Fonz. People were being hijacked in the air and on the ground and terrorists had killed Olympic athletes at Munich.

Thus endeth the second decade of me, Valinda Uffelman. I belong to the Age of Aquarius and of Helen Reddy. I have smoked marijuana and had men. I am not promiscuous, I am careful. My family don't approve of me.

I am 22 and Sheila and Cindy and I have moved to Vancouver. I have a job at St. Paul's Hospital in Richmond. Gary Campbell is my latest boyfriend. We are in to a "trial relationship" as everyone calls them nowadays. Gary is a Mountie – every Canadian girl's dream. He takes me out on night patrols and tells me about his cases. We both want very much for this to last. He has bought me a lovely ring.

I'm in a tent in the Tawassan campground. I'm sleeping on some foam rubber. I'm eating out and having my showers at the hospital. Gary and I started fighting so I just left. I couldn't afford another apartment because I had just paid my half of the one we were sharing. On my days off I go and sit in Stanley Park and play with my Tarot cards.

The death card keeps coming up. Somehow I don't care . . .

I'm back in Calgary. Alberta is booming so I've taken a real estate course and have a job with LePage Real Estate. I have top listings for this month. My big problem is that I have trouble closing a deal.

I met a man who was checking the landscaping on one of my listings. He's a landscape architect from Toronto. We talked about renovating homes for resale.

Ed and I have bigger plans than renovating houses. We're getting married. He's divorced and has a daughter Chloe. I know I love Ed but I'm not sure I can cope with a wife he is still supporting and a daughter all in the same city.

Romantically of course I am thinking of Ed's life being "broken" by the divorce and of me fixing it. Another version of "Love Story," divorce instead of death.

Today is my wedding day. I am wearing white – after all I haven't been married before. Chloe is my ring bearer. It is not as big a wedding as Mother would like – she still feels cheated about my graduation – but at least it's in a church. What Mother really wanted was a big family wedding but I told her I couldn't face all those stone-faced relatives. Of course they're not all stone-faced, only the ones who don't approve of me. In my family religion is a must, having fun a maybe. And I like fun.

We have settled on a reception at the Elks Club for our close family and our Calgary friends. Mother is putting on a reception at the farm tomorrow for the neighbors and the rest of the relatives. I hope the wind isn't blowing toward the house!

I've just seen an advertisement in the *Globe and Mail* for a landscape architect in Saudi Arabia. Saudi Arabia. Exotic, exciting, romantic, a far cry from dusty Beiseker and conservative Canada. It fulfills my wildest dreams. And we really need the money now that Ed has two households to support.

Ed is in Saudi. Bad news. His job only carries single status so I can only visit him on temporary visas. We can't get non-resident tax-free status if I stay in Canada. As if I would stay when there's a chance to "break the bonds"!

I'm in Greece. It didn't seem so strange coming here after working at Tino's Pizza. I've found an apartment in Gadalpha.

It is near the airport. My landlady's name is Kiki. I know I'm going to love Greece. I feel as though it's my natural home, my exotic home. The flowers, the buildings, the trees, the bright sunlight on white walls, the big awnings spreading coolness over the galleries. I love the sidewalk cafes, swimming in the C. Even the daylight seems to hate to leave this lovely spot.

And Kiki. She seems to have love to spare. I haven't met many people like that. Financially she is comfortable. She has her own car, her own apartment building. Her son and daughter are grown.

Her husband Theo died young in a diving accident and as a result she had fewer children than she would have liked. That is why she has empty spaces in her heart and she seems to want me to fill one, like another daughter. She always has time to sit and talk and she never expects anything of me. She has a soft love-lined face like Grandma Gilberg. She is soft for touching but I'm sure she'd fight like a lion if she had to. I feel safe with her.

I've just come back from a visit to Ed. I'm pregnant. And believe me it wasn't planned. I had applied for an administrative job in a hospital so I could stay permanently in Saudi. It looked as though I was going to get it when they gave me a medical and told me I was pregnant.

I'm still reeling from the blow. It isn't that Ed and I don't want children but we wanted to be more settled when it happened. How can I have a baby and keep trotting to and fro to Saudi? Damn!

Kiki has been a tower of strength. And she needed to be. I've been sick ever since I got pregnant. Now I'm swelling up like a bloated cow, have high blood pressure and the baby is in a breach position. I haven't been able to get to see Ed even with my new visa.

Kiki and Katerina are doing their best to get me through this. Kiki loves to sew and I have suddenly remembered my sewing from my 4-H days so we are getting things ready. I'm even working on a quilt for the baby's cot.

Kiki is making me eat healthy foods and go for walks. She laughs when the young men come and walk beside me and pretend I am "their woman." She says Greek men are very proud when their women are pregnant. It's a sexy country.

I am learning a little Greek and Kiki is learning some English. Somehow we manage to communicate. Katerina translates when we are stuck. I have learned the best way to communicate is to keep quiet and make pictures with your hands, your face, your body. Quite a switch for me who was always "running off at the mouth," as Dad used to say.

It is July, 1984 and I have a son. Ed got here in time. But I think that the person who is most thrilled about this baby is Kiki. Ed held out the baby to her and said "you are a Granny." He couldn't have said anything that would have pleased her more.

Andrew was born on a Thursday. Mother bought him a little china shoe on which was inscribed, "Thursday's child has far to go." Actually, it was my sister-in-law Karen who got it at Stettler.

I'm in Riyadh. Ed was transferred here at the end of the year. It's not as comfortable as Yanbu. Our villa is virtually on the highway so there is no place to sit outside with Andrew. It's hot and dusty and Andrew is not a very good sleeper.

After a day shut up in this cramped hot place I am ready to climb the walls. And I hate that big cloak I have to wear whenever I do get out. Ed gets frantic when I slip out without it but I just wonder how he would feel if he had to wear such a heavy cumbersome thing.

The only time I feel happy is when Ed sits down and draws up plans for our dream home. We have thought of building on the Riviera or in Greece but mostly we think of a spot I remember in B.C. The thought of that view and a cool breeze off the Pacific Ocean tugs at my heart.

I was near the bottom of the box. I picked up Valinda's last letter to us from Riyadh and reread it.

Hi everyone:. A PHL was going to the U.S. so we included this letter to be mailed from the States. We are fine – technically as of the 19th of February I am an illegal alien and may be in big T if we get stopped by security.

Andrew does a great deal of crawling backwards, sits, stands for a few seconds alone but mostly holds onto furniture. Hopefully soon, a video will be ready – friends of ours have taken pictures at all get-togethers.

As you probably know, Ed's parents are meeting us in Athens for two weeks with Chloe. We have someone here that may help me get onto Ed's resident permit in spite of the company's interference, or lack of cooperation.

I am in the midst of starting a part-time catering business to all the big American wives in the Kingdom. I've been perfecting recipes, price structures, working on my card and letterhead designs and hunting down ingredients available in Riyadh (quite a job).

There is a most fantastic French bakery which will supply me with croissants, fabulous bread, cakes and pastries. Its equal I have not seen in my travels. That will nicely take care of the fact of my non-baking attitude. I have recently attended a women's club that has a couple of thousand ladies attending – this is my advertising method. A booth and display will be set up.

Our maid has become ill and has not been able to work so we will have to find someone else. The top administrator of a large hospital has requested me to meet him for an interview – hopefully I will be working when I return from Athens next.

Love ,
Valinda, Ed and Andrew

I had thought the letter was the last of the papers in the box but under it I found two more. One was a short piece and it seemed a little smudged, as though Valinda might have been crying as she wrote it.

I've decided to leave my Uffel-mush at home this time, she wrote.

It belongs in this house because it is mostly about you who are still there. If I start another box it should be Leonard-mush for Andrew when he grows up. In case I forgot to tell you, Mother, I love you. (I'm sure if anyone bothers to read this it will be you.)

The first words of the last slip of paper in the box constricted my heart.

My favorite day of the week is Saturday. When I was a kid I loved it because school was out and I could do my hair and nails and plan a new strategy for wheedling the car out of Dad. Saturday took a lot of telephoning – if I could get the phone away from Mother and her committees – planning what Cathy and Shelly and I would do. The calls went something like this:

"Dad says I can have the car. But I have to be in by eleven."

"What else is new?"

"I'll pick you up about seven."

"Do you think Bob or Ray or Greg will be around?"

"We'll cruise and see. If not we can always listen to records. Bring your Good Luck Charm."

"Shelly has Three Dog Night."

"What are you wearing?"

"The usual. Pants. I got a new sweatshirt. Guess what's on it? 'This is the Night'."

"Keep your coat on so your Dad won't see it."

When I was grown up, Saturday night meant my friends and I were finished work for the weekend. That was when sin-bins came in handy. When my boyfriends drove out to the farm to pick me up I used to watch them top the ridge and walk out to meet them. Especially the ones Dad didn't like.

All the fun times of my life were on Saturday night.

The paper crumpled in my clenched hand. "Oh Valinda, Valinda," I wept. I cried until I thought I had no more moisture in me to make tears. I cried at the cruelty of life. Valinda, the Saturday-night girl had gone to meet her fate on a Saturday and now she was being buried on a Saturday.

I didn't go to meet Valinda's plane that Thursday night. I couldn't. Actually it was part of a harder decision I had made. I wasn't going to look at Valinda and Andrew in their coffin either.

It had been my decision that they should be buried together. All day Wednesday I had kept on doing things, filling the hours so I wouldn't have to think. Harvey watched me as long as he could and then he put his arms around me and forced me to be still.

"You're only tiring yourself out, Leah and it's not going to change anything. We've got to face the facts. We've got to make the decisions that have to be made."

He choked on the next words. "We have to have a casket – or two caskets – ready when Ed gets here."

"One," I cried. "Only one, Harvey. Valinda and Andrew can't be separated now." I didn't have to finish my thought. It was only 16 months since Andrew had left the haven of her body, not long enough for either of them to get used to being separated.

"Father O'Byrne from St. Mary's has offered us the use of the Catholic Church. The United Church is too small to hold our own family much less the neighbors."

Another of my worries jumped to the fore. "Are you sure Vaughn will make it?"

Vaughn had been the last one to see Valinda. He had visited her in Athens just before she was due to leave and afterward he and his chum Danny had gone on to the Canary Islands. We had clung to his voice when we reached him there as if somehow we could get a little closer, just one more time, to Valinda and Andrew. We hung on his words as he told us how Valinda had prepared for her trip to Saudi. They had helped her pack Andrew's stroller and toys.

"She was just like she always was, laughing and joking. She was like a schoolgirl getting ready for a Saturday night date."

By some strange coincidence, some six months earlier I had given a talk to the Calgary Toastmistress Club on "Grieving." I had based it on the ten steps of grieving. I wondered now if in some unforeseen way I had been conditioning myself for this moment.

However, while I understood about grieving, it didn't make it any easier. All I knew now was that I could not bear the thought of seeing Valinda and Andrew dead. I wanted to remember them as they had been, not as they were now.

Of course I felt guilty, cowardly, that I was letting Valinda down. Hour after hour, as the time approached for Ed to bring them home, I wrestled with the thought. Hard as I tried to keep myself occupied, it was there, tormenting me.

In the end I compromised. I didn't go. But I did choose the outfit for Valinda to be buried in. I had to do that for her. I knew she'd want to look her best. She valued her appearance. She looked good in white and she liked wearing it. I prepared her white suit. Then I added a red blouse. Only Valinda would have remembered the reason I chose that red blouse – Valinda and Mrs. Verhaest.

So I chose her burying clothes. And I read her goodbye messages.

Her girlfriends told me she had always said she would die young. And there were the tarot cards. Perhaps it was all meant to be. Perhaps she had even had a premonition. I was sure now that leaving her Uffel-mush box was her goodbye and that she intended me to read it as I had done.

I was composed when the family came home from meeting Valinda's plane. I saw Ed standing in the light from the doorway – alone – so alone – and I held out my arms to him.

Chapter 7

Kiki

✈ ✈ ✈ ✈

I am Kiki. I loved Valinda as though she were my daughter.

The day she came to me she was hot and sweaty and a little forlorn. Overweight and not accustomed to walking, she reached my place on the top of a hill needing more than the apartment she was asking for, she needed a rest.

I invited her to sit on the balcony that surrounds my apartment building. There is one at each level. I offered her a drink and she asked for a Coke, then slumped in her chair as she waited for me to get it.

She couldn't speak Greek, I couldn't speak English and my daughter Katerina wasn't home yet. That first day we managed to communicate by signs, nods, smiles and the odd word of French we each knew. Before Katerina got home I knew that her name was Valinda and I had rented her an apartment. Though she could have left once our business was settled, we sat companionably together. I had a son and a daughter but my body had been made for more, many more children and I would have had them had my husband not died so young. I even managed to tell her about him, showing her his picture and my empty bed.

She had a thirsty heart, I thought that day, just as I had but for different reasons. I guessed that she was searching for something, that there was something in her life not quite right, even though I learned, as the weeks went by, that she had a loving family and friends. She got a lot of letters and phone calls. But when little Andreas was born she said something I never forgot. She said, "Now you too have a little Madja" and she cried. There were many things she said and did that I didn't understand, even with Katerina's help.

Valinda loved the flowers at my place, the showers of crimson bougainvillea spilling over the side of the balcony. She loved the soft breeze that at our altitude blew through the balcony doors. She would lick her lips as if she could taste it. She loved to eat, especially at outdoor cafes. We had one favorite place we used to go, beside a lake. It was mostly underground but they didn't have any lakes nearby where she came from, I understood. On hot days we would go there for our evening meal and sit until the stars came through the curtain of sky.

After she became pregnant, I coaxed her to walk each day. I am a nurse and knew she needed the exercise. We would stop along the way for a drink of her beloved Coke or some ice cream. "This is the way I always wanted to live," she made me understand in the language that was slowly evolving between us.

She missed Canada I think – and her mother. But she loved her apartment in my building. She said it was her first heart's home. Actually, though, she spent more time upstairs in my apartment than her own, especially after Andreas was born.

I bought a second crib for him so he could have his afternoon naps in my place, I bought extra toys and clothes for him. He was my first grandchild. I couldn't bear to have him out of my sight. I felt blessed that Valinda was willing to share him with me. She became the sister Katerina had never had. We were all very happy together.

Sometimes I was afraid I was too happy, as I had been in the days before my husband died. I would hold Andreas so tight in my arms and pray that nothing ever happened to him.

Kiki's apartment building, where Valinda lived prior to the hijacking.

The summer was the best time. The air was always so warm and sweet from my flowers. There was the contented buzz of the bees and the flash of the hummingbirds sucking the honey from my flowers, the butterflies that Andreas tried to catch with his pudgy hands, the chatter of neighboring women who smiled and clucked at the golden-haired baby as we went by, the ship's horns in the bay and the whistle of planes coming in to land at the airport below us.

I knew they reminded Valinda of Canada and Ed. To me they were a reminder that these happy days could not always be.

I took her to the plane when her visa finally came through in November. It was raining that afternoon and the water weeping over the windshield matched my mood. It would be months before I would see Andreas again.

He was just beginning to talk. Most of his words were in Greek, to my secret delight. Just that morning he and Katerina had played a new game. He hid behind the drapes and when Katerina called "Are you there?" he answered, "na, na" meaning, "yes, yes," in Greek.

Katerina (left) and Kiki (right)

"Some way to spend a Saturday night," Valinda grumbled as we drove through the dreary rain. I understood. She always grumbled if she didn't have anything to do on a Saturday night.

"It was always special on the farm," she explained, "that's when our boyfriends came. Or we went cruising in town and met them." I had never figured out what "cruising" meant in Canada.

"I forgot to clean out my fridge," Valinda said when we got to the airport. "I left a note for Katerina asking her to do it and to keep whatever you two could use."

How like Valinda. She was always forgetting something, she lived in overdrive so much of the time. But when it came to housework she slowed down. She wasn't lazy but if she didn't like doing something she might find it easy to forget. I suspected that was what had happened with the fridge. It was a part of this "daughter" who hadn't matured yet, I thought lovingly.

I held Andreas while Valinda pushed her luggage through. As usual she had too much. I seldom saw her when she wasn't burdened down with boxes and parcels and clothes. She reminded me of that animal that carries its house on its back. Valinda carried her "house" everywhere, oblivious of things like overweight baggage on airplanes. I saw her not too adroitly palm some drachmas to the baggage clerk and knew that he would see it got on the plane. This time she had outdone herself, even including Andreas' stroller along with everything else.

When she'd finished with the main lot of her luggage, she came back for Andreas. She was still carrying far too many pieces to drag on the plane along with Andreas but somehow I knew she'd manage.

Andreas clung to me.

"Andreas, Andreas," I sobbed. "How will I do without you?"

Valinda tried to lighten the moment. "You've got a house full of his pictures," she laughed. "You'll see him everywhere you look. Besides who knows how long the Saudis will let me stay? I may be back before you know it."

I nodded tearfully and watched as Valinda trundled through the gate. Watching her, I realized this was a different girl from the one who had come to my door, hot and out of breath that first day. No, not a girl, a woman. A happy woman. Or a happier woman.

No one is ever completely happy, I reasoned. Just more or less happy than at other times. We had our own benchmark of happiness. I wasn't sure what Valinda's was but I thought she was above her benchmark in Greece. I couldn't have said why I thought this but one night I had got an inkling.

Ed had made a friend in Saudi who came originally from Greece. One night when Ed was home, Nick and his wife had come to visit. Actually they came to meet Ed's parents and Chloe, who were visiting in Athens at that time. Of course Katerina and I were invited to join the group.

The conversation slipped in and out of Greek and English, with Nick, who was completely bilingual, providing translations when needed. It soon struck me that, as well as Valinda and I had communicated, I had never before appreciated the quickness of her mind. She stimulated us all.

It was a good party. Everyone liked everyone else, and more so as the ouzo flowed. And, as is usual when the company is congenial, the conversation took curious turns and twists.

Once during a break in the conversation, Valinda asked, "Did any of you know that the sixth entry in the Columbia Encyclopedia is a place in Greece called Abdera?" She added, teasing Katerina, "And the Abderites were considered by the ancient Greeks as proverbially stupid."

"They probably told Abderite jokes instead of Newfie jokes," Ed's father chuckled.

"That's an 'in' joke in Canada," Ed explained for our benefit."

"Where did our Acropolis of Athens come in your encyclopedia?" Katerina asked.

"Page seven in the one I read," Valinda answered promptly. Turning to her in-laws, she said, "When we go to see the Parthenon tomorrow you must watch for the bronze statue of Athena. My aunt was in the Canadian Women's Army Corps and she had an Athena badge on her cap. She said thousands of girls in Canada wore them during the war and it wasn't until I came over here that she knew about the statue being here. Isn't it strange how people half across the world can be linked by a little thing like that?"

"I wonder what it is that links the greatest number of people?" Ed said curiously.

"Alcohol," said Stan Leonard. "Even enemies have been known to drink together."

"Not in Saudi," Nick answered.

"I'd say food," Stella Leonard interjected speculatively. "Everyone eats food."

"Different kinds of food," Valinda reminded her. "Some so different it would make them strangers." Then she added, "The Romans tried to link people by roads."

"Onassis the golden Greek tried to do it with ships," Ed put in.

"From the time of Alexander the Great, another famous Greek, to the time of Hitler, men have dreamed of joining peoples by power," Nick's wife reminded us.

"That's not quite the same thing though. We're talking people to people, not country to country."

"What about Billy Graham?"

As the evening wore on and more ouzo was consumed, the suggestions became more varied and the conversation more animated.

"What about water?" Nick said, his engineering mind to the fore. "Rivers flow across every continent and into every ocean. I think you could make a good case for the world being joined by water."

"Couldn't the same be said of the sky?"

"Not really. It only encloses the whole thing. We're talking about what's beneath the sky."

"So that eliminates God too."

Suddenly Valinda jumped up and waving her glass in her hand said, "I know what connects all people. It's sex. Everyone in the world, whatever color or language, knows how to make love."

Everyone laughed. "I think Valinda settled that argument," Ed said ruefully. "I can't top it anyhow."

Like the doting pseudo-mother I was, I had watched Valinda sparkle as her mind was challenged that evening. That was the core of her, I thought. Some people live in small measures but Valinda's measure must always be heaped and overflowing. She wasn't meant for "littles" only for "bigs." Just as she wasn't meant for travelling light, I thought, as I saw her still struggling to hang on to her parcels and Andreas as well.

I stayed for awhile although there was nothing we could do but smile and wave at each other while she waited to board. With a final wave I returned to my car.

I was just getting in when I spotted her purse on the seat. Snatching it up I ran back into the terminal. I met a worried

Valinda trundling Andreas and her bags back through the boarding gate. She gave a gasp of relief when she saw me.

"My passport, my money. I didn't have anything," she wailed. I was afraid I might have dropped it on the way in and someone had picked it up."

I took Andreas from her arms and tried to calm them both. After a few moments Valinda got control of herself, but not before she had hugged me fiercely.

"They're starting to board," I said. "It's lucky I hadn't started home before I saw it."

"Kiki, how could I get along without you? Thank you. Thank you for everything . . ."

The words hung in the air as she rushed back to get in line. I caught the eye of an air hostess and motioned her over. Slipping some drachmas in her hand I motioned to Valinda. She nodded that she understood and a few minutes later I saw her helping Valinda get on the plane.

I never saw Valinda and my beloved Andreas again. The next day we heard about the hijacking. Katerina was too upset to go to school. We sat in the apartment and when we were not weeping we talked as people always do of the things we remembered about Andreas and Valinda. Once we went down to Valinda's apartment and just sat there. But then I realized that in truth I felt closer to Valinda in my own apartment than in hers.

When I went into the kitchen in my mind's eye I could see Andreas climbing up on to my table sticking his little fingers into cookie dough I was stirring. I straightened the cover on his crib. Katerina lingeringly straightened the drapes behind which Andreas had hid, we looked at the pictures of him strewn about the room. We found one film that hadn't been developed yet and Katerina rushed out to get it processed.

We endured the hours just as I knew Valinda's mother and Ed must be doing. I wanted to phone Valinda's mother but I didn't want to intrude on the grief of this strange family whose daughter I thought of as my own. It was during those hours Ed phoned.

"Is Valinda there?" There was a sort of desperate hope in his voice. "I mean did she catch that plane? I thought maybe she might have missed it. She didn't confirm."

His voice stopped with a lurch. He knew my answer by my stunned silence.

"I just hoped. I've always expected her to miss a plane, she's so careless sometimes. Could you go down to the apartment, to be sure she didn't come back?"

"We've been to the apartment." Katerina who had now taken the phone said.

"Would you go again?" I could hear the pleading in his voice even from where I stood.

"I'll go down, Ed," Katerina said. "Just to be sure."

While she was gone I asked Ed where he was.

"In Riyadh. The Canadian government is in charge of things now. But they can't get me a flight out for several hours yet. They did get me a visa to leave though. You know how long those usually take." He paused and then said, "How was she when she left Kiki? Was she happy to be coming? I know she hates this town."

"She was happy, Ed."

Katerina came back and got on the phone. "There was nothing there, Ed. Only the note she left on Saturday asking me to clean out the fridge."

"Trust Valinda," Ed said brokenly.

"We must go to the florist's," I said to Katerina. "We must send some flowers."

What else is there to do when people die?

Chapter 8

Forgiveness

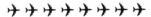

Valinda, our daughter, was buried on Saturday, her night. She would have liked the idea of saying good-bye to Beiseker on a Saturday night, I told myself. It was only we who were remembering other Saturday nights that could not bear the thought.

Everyone was there. All the neighbors and friends and relatives. The flag on the town office was at half mast and so was the one at the school. As we drove to the church I recalled the afternoons I had sat outside the schoolyard wondering what would happen to my little girl.

As I sat there in the church, looking at the closed casket, I was mercifully numb. I could see Reverend Bessy's lips moving but I couldn't hear what he was saying. I could see Father O'Byrne's lips moving but I didn't know what he was saying. I could see Joe Clark's lips moving but I didn't care what he was saying. Was he speaking as an Ottawa politician or a fellow Albertan? What did it matter what any of them said? The hijacker had had the last word.

I could sense rather than hear the commotion at the back. Was it latecomers or, more probably, the people handling the press or parking the cars who needed to slip in to get warm. It was a bitterly cold day. I was glad the priest had given Audrey Ternes and Eileen Schmaltz, members of the CWL, permission to serve hot coffee and doughnuts from the side door of the priest's house. I was glad that Vera Schmaltz and Shelly were serving coffee to the press at the school.

I was glad so many people cared so much.

I was glad when the service was over.

It was so cold they had decided to hold the graveside service privately in the church. Looking at the closed casket, in my mind's eye I could see Valinda in her white suit with Andrew resting on her breast. My shoulders shook and I clung to Harvey.

We followed the casket out of the church. We watched as they put it in the hearse. We watched as they placed the flowers over it and beside it.

But I had to look away as the hearse drove off. I couldn't bear to watch because in my mind I was not seeing it but the final few minutes at the cemetery, when they would place my loved ones in the ground. I was glad that no one would be there.

Valinda wouldn't have wanted anyone there because this was her final moment. She would know somehow that she was being laid beside her beloved Grandma Uffelman.

She would know that from now on she would always be "my little Madja."

The people of Beiseker, as people always do after one of their own is lost, had begun their process of grieving even as they made their way from the church to the Memorial Hall for lunch. At the luncheon, John Richter, mayor of Beiseker, thanked everyone for coming and said, "In a small community an event like this touches everyone. It puts everything in a different light because it hits home."

The faces of community members showed they agreed. As the meal progressed, Harvey and I overheard scraps of conversations which verbalized their pain.

"Those terrorists should be sent to burn in hell," Verle-Ann said angrily to her friends.

"Everyone is feeling rotten," said Norma Patterson, assistant principal at the school which Valinda attended for almost 12 years. "She graduated early, you know." A fellow teacher nodded sadly.

"It's hard to understand how anyone can have so little compassion," a teary-eyed Shelly said bitterly. Those around her knew she was referring to the ruthless hijackers who had killed her friend.

"I was the one who had to lower that school flag," Joe Berreth muttered to himself. "It was the hardest thing I've ever had to do, knowing why."

"Carrying that coffin was the hardest thing I ever had to do," Kenneth Leonard said to Harvey and I, speaking for the three brothers who carried the bodies for Ed.

The next day the local paper featured a write-up on the funeral.

Beiseker said a loving, dignified and tender farewell to a girl who had lived all her early life in this small farming community. And they managed to keep it a family affair despite knowing that the eyes of all Canada were upon them. But they were kindly eyes because, as one reporter from the CBC French network said, "We are here because all of Canada wants to share in the mourning for Valinda and her son."

Valinda was the kind of person who would have appreciated that. She was also the type of person who would have been particularly proud of her hometown in the way they gathered, as if with outspread arms to hold her while they said goodbye.

Among the many floral arrangements we received were two from overseas: a large wreath of Clemantis orange blossoms and white roses from the Egyptian Government bearing the message "Sympathy from Egypt" and a simple wreath from Greece with the words, "To Valinda and our beloved Andreas" from Kiki and Katerina.

As I drove home with Harvey from the funeral, I knew there was one thing yet I had to do before Valinda would really be laid to rest.

In a mistaken desire to dull my grief, my family, friends and everyone I met told me what beasts the hijackers were and what they would like to do to them. They had been crying out for revenge. And in moments of anguish I felt the same way.

Now I had to face a truth in my life. I was a professing Christian. Were these the thoughts I should be harboring?

In what now seemed an unbelievable coincidence, the psalm I had planned to read that Sunday morning one week ago now seemed like a message from Valinda.

Save me from my enemies my God,
Protect me from those who attack me,
Save me from those evil men,
Rescue me from those murderers.

How those words had knifed my heart as I reread them. But even as I writhed with the pain, I had been conscious of a voice, perhaps my preaching greatgrandfather's voice saying,

"There is more in your Bible than condemnation. There is forgiveness. Forgive others as you would have them forgive you," Christ said. "And He did just that Himself - even to the cross," the voice reminded me.

As a professing Christian, I knew what was expected of me. It was what had brought me to my room now that the funeral was over. Forgiveness. Slowly I sank to my knees by the bed. I choked back my tears and tried to pray.

"Father in Heaven, forgive me for my thoughts of revenge. And help me . . . in turn . . . to forgive . . . those terrorists – especially the one in the hospital in Malta."

Cindy Murphy
Jeann Abree
Mrs. Roseanne Linehan
Denise Dunne
Sheri Jackson
Charlotte Sullivan
Jackie Murphy
Debbie Thomas
Eileen Vinta
Tammy Collins
Connie Jowler
Andrea Coady
michelle m. Darbel
Darlene Brewer
Laurie Hogan
Marion Auget
Jill Gooac
Tina Power
Rita Morrissey
Susan Greene
Lori Parrell
Kimberly Mullins
Sorry Ezekiel

Lori Murphy
Rosanna Schlieve
Rosalie Vinta
Robin Hutton
Jo-anne Foley
Missy Power
Shelley Hoffman
Danielle Harlam
Mrs. Kathy Harren
Rhonda James
Judy Ryan Sorry
Kelly Philpott
Sherri Edwando
Paula Pynn
Veronica S. Lynen Sorry
Melanie M. Gialo sorry
Charmaine Mercer sorry
Sharon Parsons Sorry
Debbie Crapo Sorry
Tanya Kennivan Sorry
Melissa Miller
Sorry!

Chapter 9

Home

Leah hadn't come to meet the plane in Calgary. I had guessed she would find it too hard to be there knowing all the time that in another part of the terminal her daughter and grandson were being taken off the plane, being handled by strange hands. Harvey was there and Vance and Verle-Ann and Valinda's uncles and aunts. But they too had their minds on that box being unloaded out on the tarmac while we met in the room the RCMP had set aside for us.

The reporters were there but I could not talk to them. I tried but each time I tried, I'd fall apart like I had in Dhahran. I had no resistance left, the tears were always too close.

"Later," I muttered, "I'll talk to you later," and followed gratefully when Harvey motioned me out to the car.

As they drove me out to the farm I was conscious first of the peaceful black velvet sky above us, dotted with stars. It was something you always noticed in the country. Then as we drove around the Beiseker bypass, I saw how the town lights made inroads against the darkness. If those lights could hold back the darkness, couldn't people working together hold back the darkness of senseless killings like Valinda's, I wondered a little incoherently.

We drove into the farm yard and I heard the flag snapping in the wind above the house, the hot tears, the first real release of grief since it all began, poured down my cheeks.

I was finally home – in Valinda's country.

As I drank in the peace of it, the cold Alberta November wind froze the tears on my cheeks. And then I walked on the Alberta soil that, although it was frozen now, had nourished her through winter and summer over the years and would now enfold her and our baby forever.

"Goodbye Valinda. Goodbye Andrew," I whispered in my heart as Harvey opened the door of their farm home and the warm welcoming light poured out to me. Inside I could see Leah's sweet tear-drenched face, her arms outstretched to me.

As I followed the casket out of the church and then was taken with the rest of the mourners to the Memorial Hall, I realized the reporters had been as patient as they were going to be. I had to face them now.

The Town administrator, Jan Taylor, had arranged a secluded spot in the hall where I could face the cameras and the microphones. Beside me for this impromptu press conference was Joe Clark, Minister of External Affairs and my uncle.

The words that had been burning in my heart since all this began burst forth at the reporter's first question.

"Mad dogs," I cried, "That's what they are. Cowardly, ridiculous people. They must be punished. They must be stopped. Terrorism must be stopped."

"How can you stop terrorism?" came back the question I had been asking myself for days. For my answer I went back to the hours I had spent on the plane trying to come to grips with it. Then my first thought had been to use my designing skills, if not to solve the problem, at least to alleviate its terrible potential.

"Maybe there could be a way for the captain to inject knockout gas into the oxygen system, putting everyone, including hijackers, safely to sleep. Or maybe high-suction fans could be installed to draw off smoke in a fire. Why couldn't there be a mechanism enabling the pilot to blow out all the windows and emergency doors, immobilizing the plane and permitting easier access?"

"And then there's security," I went on. "How good is it? When I travelled to Saudi from Athens, I used to smuggle aboard a bottle of ouzo or a few beer, enough for a three-hour flight. It was harmless, for my own consumption on the plane but I should not have been allowed to check it through. If I could smuggle liquor on board what else could be taken on?"

"Each passenger is allowed to check up to 20 kilograms of luggage. But Valinda travelled with an unbelievable amount of paraphernalia – up to 70 kilos of luggage plus car seats and strollers and all kinds of other things. To avoid paying penalties or to avoid being held up as she boarded, she would slip the ticket agent five or ten dollars. Again, a harmless act. But if she could break the rules so easily, terrorists certainly could break them just as easily."

"Finally, there must be ways of making airports and aircraft less vulnerable. Would it help to circulate photos of known terrorists or to alert travellers to dangers like abandoned luggage?"

By the time the interview was over I knew I hadn't solved any problems. But I had solidified an idea that had been forming in my mind. Before I would know any peace I would have to go back to the source of my agony. Back to Malta. They had one of the hijackers in custody. They had to have a trial or at least a hearing.

There were questions I had still to ask. Questions like why did the Egyptian troops storm the plane the way they did? It seemed clear their explosives were much too powerful so why did they indulge in what had really been unnecessary force? Were they right when they claimed that the grenades thrown by the hijackers started the fire or were they just trying to put a better light on their own actions? I must go back to Malta. I must attend those hearings.

I was assuming, of course, that a hearing would take place. As the months dragged by I became more and more unsure of this. Joe Clark's Department of External Affairs sent firm requests for information but nothing happened. I made trips to both Athens and Malta trying to get information and got no answers. It was as though a curtain had been pulled down over the whole affair. It didn't seem conceivable that this hijacker they had in custody wasn't going to be tried and punished but there was little to indicate otherwise at that time.

I finally managed to locate Abram the reporter I had talked to in Malta. He was as angry as I was that nothing was being done. By now we were both of the opinion that there was a cover-up going on.

It was rumored that both the Egyptians and Maltese were holding investigations in secret. There was talk the Americans had played a larger part than they wanted known in the bombing of the plane. It was said the Americans were determined to call a halt to the rash of terrorist attacks and were fighting back. It was, the rumors seemed to be implying, just my misfortune that my family happened to be among the sacrificial lambs in the Americans' first attempt at playing hard ball with terrorism.

I could understand them fighting back. In fact, like most people, I felt it was time. But all that didn't make losing my family any easier.

The day came when I realized I couldn't suspend my life indefinitely. I had to go home and start making a living.

Abram promised to smuggle out a transcript, if and when, a hearing was held. It wasn't much but it seemed the best I could hope for.

Chapter 10

The Malta Hearings

During the months following the hijacking, the ghastly hulk of the death plane still sat at the edge of the Malta runway. Only the blood-soaked tarmac and the floor of the hangar where the victims had been placed to await identification by their relatives had been mopped up.

Day after day, the diluted rays of a wintry sun played bleakly over the ghostly reminders of the dead but did little to heal either the trauma suffered by the Maltese people at what had happened in their midst or the wounds, real or emotional, of those who had been caught in the vortex of horror that rain-soaked night in November.

Around the world the grieving relatives tried to cope with their loss of loved ones.

In Canada, on their snowbound farm in Beiseker, Leah and Harvey Uffelman somehow managed to get through Christmas. Ed, feeling closer to Valinda and Andrew through them, also managed, with their help, to stumble through this emotion-wrenching season. They did it for each other by Leah recalling for Ed and perhaps for herself, Valinda's first Christmases while Ed described everything he could remember of Andrew's one and only Christmas.

In Greece, Kiki and Katerina looked through tear-filled eyes at Andrew's many pictures strewn about the apartment and remembered all his sweet ways.

In Israel, the United States, England, Greece, Egypt, the Philippines and all the other places where families had lost relatives or friends on that flight, the pain continued. Pain which as time went on was augmented by the nagging thought that no one seemed to be trying to find out what had happened or why.

Why wasn't anyone being punished?

The preliminary hearings to determine whether Omar Mohammed Ali Rezaq should be committed for trial began on

January 6, 1986 and lasted until April 3, 1987. Altogether the Lebanese-born Palestinian appeared more than 30 times before a magistrate in preliminary hearings held within the secure bastions of Fort St. Elmo, in Malta. Equally secure accommodation was provided for him at Corradino Civil Prison. Always, day and night, the hijacker was guarded by relays of specially trained men.

His first court appearance was on December 12th, 1985 when he was arraigned before Magistrate Dr. C. Farraguia Sacco. Rezaq, claiming to be a driver of no fixed address, was charged on 16 counts including charges of causing the death of Scarlett Rogenkamp, an American and Nitzan Mendelson, an Israeli woman, plus grievous injuries to others. Rezaq pleaded "not guilty" to all charges.

On January 14, 1986, Police Inspector Daniel Gatt, for the Prosecution, requested the Court add one more charge, the willful intention of harming or killing the pilot, Capt. Hani Galal. The request was granted. Rezaq pleaded not guilty to that too.

The hearings lasted 15 months. They required several extensions of time to complete, each one authorized by the President of the Republic. In all more than 200 pages of transcript was compiled.

Chapter 11

The Doctor

I, Abram, the reporter who had been on the tarmac the night the plane with its cargo of dead and about-to-die passengers landed at Luqa Airport, had been assigned the job of covering the hearings.

It was an assignment I both wanted and dreaded. I wasn't sure I could go through all that agony again. And yet, I too, felt I must know what had really happened that dreadful night.

In actual fact my reporting of this tragic episode which had changed the face of airline hijacking began when I was sent to the hospital to interview the injured passengers.

I talked to Patrick Scott Baker, an American and Capt. Hani Galal, the pilot and Anthony Lyons, an Australian. It was he who told me that one of the hijackers was in the hospital.

Of course I tried to interview the hijacker, Omar Mohammed Ali Rezaq but the hospital staff and the police prevented it. All I got was an unsatisfactory glimpse of his face.

Now in the courtroom, I saw him face to face.

He was between 29 and 30, of average height. He had a long face, a long nose, black hair and dark eyes. His eyes were his most arresting feature.

✈ ✈ ✈

Dr. Victor Buhagiar, a young houseman at St. Luke's, was the first person allowed on the hijacked plane in Malta. He was the last witness on the third day of Rezaq's hearing.

Up until now the testimony, most of it preliminary, had been from witnesses involved only in the hijacking aftermath. None of them had been closer to the plane than the grass along the tarmac.

For example, P.C. Joseph Brincat of the Police Special Mobile Squad, who with his men had concealed themselves as best they could in the grass had testified that there was no special lighting at the scene, like searchlights on the aircraft. Only the airliner's lights were on. He had added that it was raining heavily but there were periodic lightning flashes which almost seemed to explode against the exterior of the plane.

Professor Victor Sultana of St. Luke's had described Rezaq's wounds when he was examined in the hospital. He said they were quite extensive. He had an abrasion on his left eyebrow and two chest wounds. One of the chest wounds was one centimetre long at the level of the second rib on the left side of the chest. He also had air under the skin.

The second wound, also one centimetre long, was on the left buttocks. This may have been caused when a missile or a cutting object scaled the lower part of the back. An X-ray of the chest revealed air and blood in the left chest. When he operated on Rezaq, Prof. Sultana said he found four puncture wounds in the left lung, two in the upper lobe and another two in the lower lobe. It seemed that a missile or projectile had entered the body from in front and left from the back. It pierced the lung and was deflected by about 10 centimetres after hitting the sixth rib on its way out. There were two litres of blood in the chest as a result of the wounds. One litre consisted of blood clots. The blood pass was arrested and wounds were treated. The man's condition then continued to improve.

Two more witnesses added to the unfolding picture of what had happened outside the plane that night.

Police Inspector Gatt testified he had interviewed passengers such as Patrick Scott Baker and Tony Lyons in the hospital.

Prof. Marie Therese Camilleri testified that although 60 people had died in the incident, 62 death certificates were issued. This was because two dead women were pregnant and a certificate was issued on each of the two fetuses.

A tremor went through the courtroom as Dr. Buhagiar took the stand. Only he could tell us what the interior of the doomed plane looked like as its doors were opened for the first time after landing. Those of us in the courtroom had an eerie sense of entering the plane with him.

Dr. Buhagiar testified that on November 23, 1985, he was on duty at St. Luke's when he was told to go to the airport together with Dr. Anthony Mifsud. They arrived at Luqa about 10:30 p.m. Dr. Vincent Moran, the Minister of Health, told them that one of them had to board the Egyptian airliner. Dr. Buhagiar said he went to the aircraft in an ambulance accompanied by a nurse, a driver and three members of the Police Task Force.

From the Trial Transcript:

The nurse and I alighted from the ambulance, intending to board together. We were stopped when someone from the aircraft, using a loud-hailer shouted in English, "Only the doctor can board." I moved forward reluctantly.

I stood at the foot of the mobile stairway that was brought and waited for the door to be opened.

I sucked in my breath as the door rolled back. My first glimpse of the inside of the plane was shocking. What I saw was a hooded man holding a pistol pointed at a hostess.

The hooded man waved the pistol indicating that I was to come up the steps and enter the plane. I did.

There was a heavy, almost acidic odor inside the plane. I have never smelled fear but if I did I think it would smell like that. There was a film-like quality to the light in the cabin, not unlike a party where everyone is smoking. I couldn't see any cigarettes so it may have been the gunsmoke still hanging in the heavy air.

As I entered I could see a man lying face up on the first seat to my right. He had an oxygen mask on his face but showed no signs of life. I went closer and examined him. He was dead.

A man in a uniform whom I learned later was the pilot said in English, "What is the condition of this man?"

"Grievously injured," I answered. I knew of course that he was dead, but I was afraid to say so.

The man in uniform again asked the condition of the man and I was forced to say, "He is dead."

I then got up the courage to look around the aircraft. I could see that it was full and nearly everyone was seated. Standing nearby was the hooded man I had seen holding the gun pointed at the hostess. He had moved closer to me while I was examining the dead man and that was why I had been afraid to admit he was dead.

There was another hooded man, this one standing between the middle and back part of the plane. The passengers sitting in the second row motioned me with their eyes to look under the front seat on the other side. There I saw another wounded man. He was lying face down. I asked the man with the pistol if I could examine the second body. He waved his pistol in a way that seemed to mean "no."

There were two air hostesses sitting on seats near the front. They were moaning, one complaining about a pain in her back and the other about a pain in her leg. I went to examine them but before I could do so, the man in uniform grabbed one up pick-a-back and carried her off the plane. I took the arm of the other one and began to follow him.

The hooded man watched to see what I was doing and then waved me out of the aircraft.

The testimony that Dr. Buhagiar had just given would appear in the transcript, I knew, couched in the legalese that I was hearing in the courtroom. In fact all the testimony of this trial, which I judged would be long because of the many witnesses to be called, would be in the legal jargon so dear to the hearts of lawyers.

But the "transcript" I would be sending to my Canadian friend, Ed Leonard, I determined would be in mercifully condensed form and if it was humanly possible to mitigate the horrifying details, in words with which a grieving husband could cope.

Chapter 12

The Stewardesses

Hana Elderbi and Ashan Atia Mohamed were the first to know that this was a hijacking. On January 30th, 1986, Hana Elderbi was called as a witness.

From the Trial Transcript:

I am employed as an air hostess with EgyptAir. On November 23 I was on a flight from Athens to Cairo. We left Athens sometime in the evening.

Ashan and I were the first to come into actual contact with the hijackers.

Take-off was normal and when the "Fasten seat belts" sign was switched off I saw one of the passengers trying to open the cockpit door. I opened the toilet door for him. He went inside and after a few seconds he came out holding a bomb in his right hand. With his left hand he opened the cockpit door.

We had done all the usual things, made sure the plane door was securely locked, sat down in our usual seats facing the passengers during take-off and then gone through the safety drill. I even had time to check on the woman with the baby and all the luggage. She looked comfortable on the front seat where I had placed her. We exchanged smiles.

I went into the pantry area to start preparing the meals while Ashan got her newspaper trolley loaded. That was when the man who had gone to the toilet suddenly bounded out again and after a warning glare at me, charged into the cockpit. He was carrying a bomb and a revolver.

At the same time another man, about four rows down, leapt out of his seat. He had a bomb in one hand and a pistol in the other.

"Sit down," he shouted, waving his gun at Ashan and me. We did as we were told.

He went to the front and stood looking at the passengers. He glanced at the woman and baby in the front. The child was squirming to get out of his mother's arms, wanting to get down and move around, I guessed.

The hijacker must have realized that too. Suddenly he said to Ashan, "Order the passengers from the first four rows to the back. Tell them to come out of their seats one by one."

Ashan did as she was told. Warily the passengers began to move from their seats. One of the first was the woman and her child. She was still trundling her luggage and I wished I could help her.

The hijacker searched each one and asked for the passports. He waited impatiently as the woman tried to get hers out while at the same time balancing the baby on her hip and moving her luggage from arm to arm. I was afraid he might strike her with the gun in his hand, because she was taking so long. But he didn't. Perhaps he had a child of his own.

There were two women following the woman and child but after seeing their passports, he got very angry and pushed them around before he seated them. He did not let them go to the back. He grabbed one of them by the hair.

The next to be searched was a security guard. I knew there were four on the plane but this was the only one I could recognize. He had flown with us from Cairo. Once the hijacker realized the man was a security guard, he got angry again and began to handle him roughly. In the end he tied his hands behind his back and made him lie face down on the floor in the aisle.

"He then asked for my passport and searched me. After he had finished, he looked me in the eye and said, 'Where are the other security guards?'

"I don't know."

"How many are there on the plane?"

"I don't know."

His eyes bored into me. "I warn you," he said, "If I find another security guard that you haven't told me about, I will kill you."

When I still didn't tell him, he pushed me into one of the four front rows, where there were already three passengers. The hijackers' plan seemed to be to move the passengers forward to the emptied front rows as they were searched. We took the arm off the seat but there still was not enough room so I hung over into the aisle.

The hijacker continued down the cabin still body-searching each passenger. I dreaded for him to find another security guard. I was afraid he meant it when he said he'd shoot me.

About halfway down the cabin he did find another security guard. From where I sat, I could only partly see what was going on but suddenly the man he had just ordered out of his seat to be searched, took out a gun and shot. At almost the same moment the hijacker shot back.

The two of them fell to the floor. Then gunfire seemed to break out all over. The hijacker who had gone into the cockpit jerked open the door and began shooting at the security guard who had opened fire. I think there were shots from the back of the plane also.

I was hit in the back by one of the shots.

All the passengers had put their heads down behind the seats to escape the bullets and so did I.

The oxygen masks fell down. To put them on we had to raise our heads from behind the seats where we had been trying to hide. Putting them on seemed to distract everyone's attention for a few moments, even the hijackers. I think I was moaning a little from the pain in my back but I could still see what was going on.

Suddenly the hijacker who, from the cockpit door had put more bullets into the already bleeding security guard, came out to the front of the cabin and started waving his gun around. He seemed to be taking over from the hijacker that had been shot.

He walked down the aisle to where the wounded hijacker was and ordered two passengers to carry him to the front and put him on a seat. I instinctively got up and put an oxygen mask on the injured hijacker. It was part of my job. The security guard was left in the aisle.

The hijacker from the cockpit now continued with the body searches and with collecting passports. In the meantime he appeared to have discovered another security guard in the cockpit who was dressed as a crew member and he now ordered him to help.

A doctor came on board.

I couldn't move after that. I was very tired and I kept my head down all the time. I don't remember much until the Captain picked me up and carried me off the plane. I remember that as we reached the door of the plane the fresh air revived me enough that I could see the accused standing there with his gun on us.

Under cross-examination Hana Elderbi said she had only spoken with the accused for a very short time before he went into the cockpit. "But I am sure that it was the accused," she said. Apart from the time the two met near the cockpit door at the beginning of the flight, the witness said she never saw the face of the accused again. She said she was not sure whether the accused wore a mask or not when he shot the security guard on the floor "but when I left the plane I saw his eyes," the witness said, adding "that was enough."

Ashan Atia Mohamed was the next witness called. She testified sitting down because she suffers from varicose veins.

Ten minutes after take-off I was pushing the trolley down the aisle distributing newspapers. About halfway down the length of the plane, I felt someone behind me who seemed very nervous. I could see that it was a man wearing glasses. He seemed fat with a reddish, chubby face. He wore a moustache.

Suddenly he shoved me aside and grabbing the trolley, pushed it to the rear. He had a gun in his hand. I turned to complain about this "madman," as I thought he was, to the Chief Stewardess but as I did so I saw a tall, thin man with a thin face at the front of the cabin also with a gun in his hand.

I gasped. I realized at that moment that this was a hijacking.

I started toward the front of the cabin but I had only gone a few steps when the man with the gun shouted, "Sit down."

I couldn't find a seat so kept on walking to the front to find one. He thought I was disobeying him and kicked me into the seat I finally found. Later, Hana came and sat next to me.

The hijacker ordered all the men to take off their ties. He spoke in Arabic but made gestures to show what he meant. He waved his gun at me and told me to tell the passengers, in English, what he wanted them to do.

He gave the orders in a nervous manner. In Arabic he said, "Tell all the passengers not to speak. Tell all the passengers to take out their passports and hold them in their right hand. Tell them to put both hands on their heads."

I repeated his orders twice in English. I wanted to be sure all the passengers heard.

The passenger searched before me was an Egyptian farmer. I could tell because he wore the *beba*. The hijacker saw that he was an Egyptian and did not treat him as roughly as he had the Israeli women.

When he got to me he said, "Give me your passport."

"I do not have it, " I answered. "It's in my handbag at the back of the plane."

"Go and get it."

As I reached the back I saw again the man who had pushed me down the aisle.

I returned to the front and handed over my passport. As he read it the hijacker said suspiciously, "You are an Egyptian and called Ashan?"

I said,"Yes."

"Do you know where the security guards are seated on the plane?"

"No."

His eyes looked straight into mine. Then he told me to sit in the third row. Three men were already there. I had to sit partly on the arm of the aisle seat. I guess that is why I got hit when the shooting started. I felt the pain in my left thigh and hip.

My first thought was to put my head down to avoid being hit again. I was in real pain. I pulled up my skirt and saw the wound. I was very frightened.

After awhile when I had calmed down and there was no more shooting. I raised my head and looked around.

I saw a pair of legs sticking out of the first row of seats. I realized it was the hijacker who had kicked me and took my passport. I saw that the fourth hostess was trying to distribute food. I don't remember much that happened after that until we landed in Malta. I was busy trying to stop the bleeding in my leg.

I can't remember whether I saw the hijacker come out of the cockpit before or after we landed. I was very upset. He was not the same terrorist as had pushed my trolley cart. This hijacker's face was covered but I could see his eyes. They were dark brown.

✈ ✈ ✈

Under cross-examination Ashan testified, "At the hospital I was asked to identify the terrorist. Before I identified him I took a photograph given me by the Police and covered the upper and lower parts of his face, leaving his eyes showing. I was then certain that the man in the picture was the hooded terrorist. I can identify this man as the accused. I can remember his eyes. He had a particular look by which one can single him out.

Chapter 13

The Captain

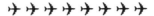

Captain Hani Galal made the first pleas on behalf of the passengers.

> *Valetta, Malta (UPI-AP-Reuters). Four people were killed yesterday after hijackers commandeered an EgyptAir jetliner and forced it to land in Malta with nearly 100 people on board, Malta television and U.S. officials said.*
>
> *The victims included one of the hijackers and an Egyptian security guard but the identities of the other two and the circumstances of the deaths weren't immediately known, U.S. State Department spokesman Don Cofman said.*
>
> *Maltese television said the plane touched down at Luqa Airport at 2:16 p.m. MST with "some dead people on board" and the hijackers threw out one body, apparently to back demands for refueling.*
>
> *A man identifying himself as one of the hijackers told airport officials shortly after landing that "I am going to look for another American passport."*
>
> *Reporters listening in on communications between the Boeing 737 and Maltese authorities said a man who identified himself as Hani Galal, the captain of the plane, was heard saying, "Another passenger is being prepared for execution. I demand fuel. I do not want any more bloodshed. I am responsible for the safety of passengers and crew." Later a ham radio operator on the Mediterranean island, said he heard the captain say, "They've killed another one."*

I am Captain Hani Galal and I am employed as an airline captain by EgyptAir. Before that I served for seven years in the Egyptian Air Force.

My co-pilot, Emad Bahey and I were in the cockpit, along with one of the security guards dressed as a crew member.

I always had a good feeling when I set out on a flight. I could picture all the normal, accustomed things going on in the cabin behind me. Most of the planes I flew were economy, like this one, so there was no partitioning off of the passengers. They were all there together in one long, comfortable cabin, three seats on each side and two at the very back in order to make room for the oxygen tanks. The long corridor stretched back, empty until the stewardesses started doing their work or the passengers started using the toilets.

Sometimes I would turn the controls over to the co-pilot just for the pleasure of walking back through the plane to be sure "my flock" were comfortable. That's how I thought of them. My job as a boy had been to herd my father's sheep. I loved to sit on a hillside watching them contentedly dozing in the sun. My passengers were usually content once they had got through the hassle of getting aboard and getting their luggage stored. They relaxed, satisfied to let me do the work of getting them to their destination. Some of them read, some put their heads back and closed their eyes and others carried on low-voiced conversations, their words drowned out except to their companions, by the noise of the plane.

Those were the pictures in my mind before the hijacker burst into the cockpit that night and for all time destroyed my vision of a contented planeload of passengers.

From the Trial Transcript:

"The plane is hijacked. Change your course to Malta," he shouted in Arabic while waving a grenade in his hand.

His voice was high and excited. My first thought was to calm him down. "I am not going to resist you," I said placatingly.

"Don't talk to anybody via radio and change your course immediately to Malta." We were speaking Arabic. I discovered later that the accused understood some English so from then on I was careful.

"If we change the course we have to change the altitude," I said. "And to do that we have to contact Athens to change the direction or else we might collide with another aircraft. Also we don't have enough fuel to reach Malta. We have enough to go to Italy or return to Athens."

"You have to go to Malta. I don't want to go to Italy."

I turned back to the controls, hoping the fuel would hold out.

"Keep a sharp lookout," I said to Emad. "We're crossing air routes. We don't want to collide with another plane."

"Call Athens and get me someone who speaks Arabic," the accused hijacker demanded.

They put EgyptAir's catering manager at the Athens station on the air. I recognized his voice.

"How do you use this?" the hijacker asked, pointing at the radio. I showed him where to press on the microphone to send a message.

He began making his statement. The first words were: "The Egyptian Revolutionary Organization has seized flight 737." I did not listen to the rest. It was the same rubbish we are always hearing over the radio in this part of the world, all about imperialism and so on.

After he made his statement he put on his hood. It was green and made of wool and covered his head to his neck, revealing only the upper lip, nose, eyes and eyebrows, through a hole. It was green.

Instead of listening to him, I used my time trying to think of ways I might save my passengers.

"Tell Athens we are changing course to Gozo," I instructed Emad. I hoped Athens would guess that our destination was Malta. I had not been able to get through to Malta although I had tried several times. I hadn't even been able to reach them through other planes. I wanted to let the Maltese controllers know about the hijacking so they could take the necessary precautions.

"How many hijackers are on the plane?" I now asked, wondering how many we would have to contend with.

"You will find out," he snapped.

I found out sooner than I wanted. Emad and I literally leaped out of our seats when the first shots were fired. We tried to get to the passenger cabin but the hijacker was on the observer's seat behind us and we were trapped. He had flung the cockpit door open at the first shot and was now shooting into the cabin. He just sat there on the observer's seat and kept pumping bullets into the passenger area.

One of the bullets, perhaps more, had hit the fuselage. The aircraft began depressurizing at a dangerous rate.

"We have to go down," I said. We had been cruising at 35,000 feet. We started going down and finally levelled out at 14,000. Now I had another problem. Flying at 14,000 takes a lot more fuel than at 35,000. While I might have been only half serious when I told the hijacker we didn't have enough fuel to get to Malta, now I knew it was deadly serious.

The accused had gone out of the cockpit for a few minutes after the shooting but now he was back on the observer's seat. I got his attention and pointed at the fuel gauge. "I don't think we can make it to Malta. We've got to go to Italy. It's on our right."

"Show me the map," he answered. The co-pilot held it up for him to see and I pointed out our present position.

"How far away is the Jamahiriya?" the accused asked. He was referring to Libya.

"Benghazi is to our left," I said.

"No, Tripoli."

"We are nearer to Malta," I said resignedly.

"We will proceed to Malta then," he said.

"What if Malta won't allow us to land? We have a better chance of being allowed to land in Italy."

"We will *make* Malta allow us to land."

Malta denied us permission to land – three times. By the third refusal I was getting desperate.

"Relay my request to land to the highest authorities in Malta," I demanded.

"In the name of humanity," I pleaded, when I got someone, "Let us land." I glanced anxiously out of the cockpit window. We were in the midst of a thunderstorm and except for the flashes of lightning, it was black outside. I could picture the sea boiling beneath us in the darkness. If I ditched the plane we would all drown.

Whether it was my words or the fear in my voice, or just because I had appealed to the higher ups, I finally got permission to land. My next thought was to see if this landing might help me in outwitting the hijackers.

"I'm going to land heavy," I warned the co-pilot in a low voice. "Maybe it will throw the hijackers off balance enough for the passengers to overpower them."

I did not use much of a reverse thrust. My intention was to exert a great amount of heat on the wheels so that the tires would be deflated. But my ploy failed. I could tell this when I felt the normal steering.

"Tell the authorities we want to park the plane in a remote place," the hijacker ordered.

"They want to land where they can't be reached easily," I told the tower. The tower indicated an area which was empty.

"I could see some small huts off to the side and I attempted to stop the aircraft near them. But the accused spotted them as well and ordered me on."

"Stop there," he said, indicating a clear spot.

He was right behind me with the grenade still in his left hand and his right hand, with the revolver in it, resting on the back of my seat with the gun pointed at my neck, so I didn't argue.

The spot he chose was where the storming finally took place.

The hijacker took a cardboard pack out of his righthand jacket pocket and taking some rounds of ammunition from it, reloaded the empty chambers.

While he was doing this he said, "Can we fly again with this plane or does it need fixing?"

"It needs fixing. Some of the bullets hit the fuselage."

"OK, tell them we need fuel and an engineer to fix the plane. And say that the engineer must come alone and that the fuel must be brought to us in the shortest possible time."

"Hold on," the tower answered. "We will consider the request."

While we waited for their answer I tried to think of a way to find out more about the hijackers and what their intentions had been.

"Where did you really want to go when you took over the plane?" I asked.

"What difference does it make?"

"Well, if I knew where you wanted to go and if you still plan on going there once we get the fuel I would know how much fuel we needed."

"Tell them to fill it to the top," he answered curtly.

I said that to speed things up I needed his co-operation and part of that was letting me go out to the cabin and see how the passengers were faring. One way or another the hijacker had, from the start, managed to keep me from seeing what was going on behind me. At first he had done it by keeping the cockpit door closed. Since the shooting, the door had been open but he had managed to keep himself between me and the cabin so I had no idea what had really happened out there.

"Get them to send the fuel and I'll let you go out," he answered.

"It might help us to get the fuel if you released the women and children."

"I am going to release the Egyptian women."

When more time had passed and we hadn't got any answer from the tower, he took a different tack.

"Tell them to send an ambulance and a doctor."

I did this and then I stood up and said, more forcibly this time, "I want to see the passengers' cabin." This time he let me.

I shall never forget the sight that met my eyes. Passengers were cowering in their seats, food was falling out of the meal trolleys, pieces of carry-on luggage had slid into the aisle, some of the overhead luggage compartments had fallen open and blankets were hanging down, newspapers were strewn about the aisles and hanging over the arms of aisle seats, a passenger was leaning her head against a window, tears running down her cheeks, a briefcase was lying open almost at my feet with passports and men's ties falling out of it and there were – *bodies*.

On the floor was the injured security guard. Lying on his back on the first row of seats to my right was one of the hijackers. He had an oxygen mask on. He was occupying two and a half seats and his legs dangled from the edge of the seat from the knee downwards.

"He is one of ours," the accused said in a tight voice.

As I passed down the aisle the passengers pleaded, "Where are we?" Some were speaking Greek, some Egyptian and some English. But the words and the look in their eyes all asked the same thing.

"We are in Malta," I answered in several languages. "Everything is going to be alright."

I stumbled back into the cockpit and sank horrified into my seat. What could I do?

"Tell the control tower that if an unauthorized person approaches the aircraft, I will blow it up," he said.

I was not surprised when he added, "Only the doctor can come on board."

The accused held a gun on one of the hostesses as I opened the plane door for the doctor. It was the first time the door had been opened since we left Athens. I always enjoyed the end of a flight and the doors being opened, the passengers eager to get off but still taking time to thank me for a safe journey. But there was no joy in opening the door this flight because no passengers were getting off.

I looked warningly at the nervous young doctor and spoke only in English as I showed him the hijacker on the front seat.

"Is he dead?" I asked in a low voice.

"Grievously injured," the doctor said, avoiding my eyes.

He looked dead to me so I repeated my question. "Is he dead?"

"Yes, he is dead." I noticed then that the accused was standing at his shoulder and guessed that the doctor had been afraid to tell the truth about the dead hijacker.

The doctor moved toward the stewardesses who were moaning in pain.

"Leave them," the accused snapped.

After a moment, whether it was because he now knew the hijacker was dead or simply an erratic change of mind, he suddenly shouted, "Leave the plane!" and waved his gun at the doctor. The doctor looked both relieved and surprised. He must have been wondering, as I was, why the hijacker had demanded his presence in the first place.

As the doctor started to obey his orders I decided to do something about the stewardesses.

"I'm going to evacuate the injured stewardesses," I said to the accused. I didn't wait for him to answer. I just picked one up, put her on my shoulder and walked out of the plane. The other one quickly followed me, along with the doctor. When they were safely in the ambulance I went back inside the aircraft.

I didn't want to go back, I could easily have jumped into the ambulance and probably got away. But all that I stood for as a pilot stopped me. I was responsible for the passengers in that plane. Perhaps I was remembering a golden-haired little boy I had seen through the cockpit window as his mother carried him on board.

I went back on the plane, closed the door and returned to my seat in the cockpit where the accused was once more seated on the observer's seat.

"You could have fled," he said. "But you came back."

"You knew I had to," I answered. "It is part of my job."

"Yes, I knew you would come back," he said.

I felt as though I had gained his confidence by my actions. I hoped I could use it for the benefit of the passengers.

"Will you put the safety catch on your grenade?"

"I have already done that."

"Please ask your colleagues to do the same."

"All right."

I again asked, "Will you let the women and children go?" He called the Chief Stewardess and asked for the passports of the Egyptian women. He told her to call out their names.

I stood at the plane door. As each women passed I said in Egyptian "Hurry in case he changes his mind. Run out of range as soon as you get off." One woman stopped on the passenger steps and said, "My husband is in there." I almost pushed her down the stairs.

The accused then asked the Chief Stewardess for the Filipino passports. I think there were seven Filipino women. I again hurried them off the plane.

The accused then said, "That's all," brushed his hands together in a dismissive gesture and closed the door himself.

It had been a long session, so the sitting was suspended for a few minutes. Captain Galal asked for a drink of water and got up and stretched. Everyone but the accused moved around, easing the tension. When the pilot returned to the stand, he asked to make a statement. He said:

Sometimes I get so angry that I forget in what order things happened. I have just been reminded that before he let the women off the accused disposed of the wounded security guard, the one who had started the gunplay by shooting the hijacker. It shocked me so much, I guess I didn't want to remember it. The security guard was in actual fact the first person to be thrown off the plane.

The accused ordered two of the other security guards, the one who had been in the cockpit in a crew uniform and a bearded one called Nabil, to drag the wounded guard outside the plane onto the passenger step platform. I followed them and knelt down to feel his pulse. It was still beating.

"He is still alive," I said, looking at the accused's gun trained on him. "There's no need to kill him. He's helpless."

"He shot one of us," the accused answered angrily. "He should bleed to death. He should die."

"You are Arabic," I said. "It is wrong for us to kill a wounded man." Deliberately, the accused pointed his gun at the wounded guard's neck and chest and shot him at close range.

I knelt down again and put my hand on the guard's neck pulse. To my surprise he was still alive.

"Is he dead?" the accused asked.

"Yes, of course," I answered. I lied because I didn't want the accused to shoot him again.

"Throw him off the steps," the accused said.

I grabbed the man's feet and turned his legs towards the opening of the platform and pushed him towards the tailside. He landed on the tarmac. I stood so the accused could not see him move.

We went back to the cockpit. The accused seemed to be growing increasingly restless.

"Ask them again for fuel," he said irritably.

This time when I asked, I added, "I am saying this with a gun at my head." They refused once more.

I told him warily, "They say they won't give you the fuel until all the women and children are released."

"I released the Egyptians and Filipinos. That is enough." I could feel his anger rising.

"If we do not have the fuel truck here within 15 minutes, I will shoot a passenger," the accused shouted angrily.

He stormed out of the cockpit and returned with an Israeli passport in his hand.

"This is an Israeli passport on an Egyptian airliner. There was a time when an Israeli would never have dared to approach an Arab country. When I was in the Athens airport last night I saw an Israeli girl buying an air ticket to Cairo. An Israeli girl can go to Cairo but I cannot."

"I fought against the Israelis in the 1973 war," I said, trying to calm him. "The co-pilot here is the son of an Egyptian general who was wounded in the 1973 war."

"Where are the heroes now who fought in that war?" he cried out bitterly. "They are no longer controlling things in Egypt. They sold out at Camp David. They committed treason in that agreement."

By talking to him I had hoped to take his mind off the threat to kill a passenger in 15 minutes. But to my horror I realized he was actually counting the minutes. I couldn't believe anyone would only take 15 minutes to think about killing someone.

When the 15 minutes were exactly up he went out of the cockpit. This time he left the door open. He gave the Israeli passport to Shadia, the Chief Stewardess.

"Call out that name," he ordered. The name was Artzi Tamar. The girl came out of her seat willingly. She obviously thought she was going to be released as the other women were.

I shuddered. I knew what he intended to do.

He grabbed her by the shoulder and moved towards the plane's entrance door. It was only when the girl was on the platform with the gun pointed at her that she seemed to realize he was going to shoot. She screamed and stepped backward.

From the cockpit window I could see the gun almost touching her face. The accused stepped closer and slapped her face. She shrieked, "No! No!" and turned her head to the right.

He shot her in the face.

The girl fell down on the platform. He kicked her off.

I grabbed the microphone and shouted into it. "He's really shot a passenger! Please do something before he kills another one!"

The accused closed the plane's door and returned to the observer's seat in the cockpit. He was very calm.

Exactly 15 minutes later, he left the cockpit and called another girl. From her name, Nitzan Mendelson, I assumed that she too was Israeli.

This time the victim knew what was in store for her. She did not answer when her name was called.

He ordered the stewardess to get her. The stewardess said, "There is another Israeli girl passenger. Please, she has to come out." I saw a girl trying to hide herself. She put her head down behind the front seat. By making these movements she identified herself. The hostess walked down to her and said, "Please come out." When she refused the accused ordered two passengers to bring her out by force. She was crying and grabbing the seat and pleading, "Please, no."

They managed to pull her out. They dragged her to the accused and he made her kneel down in front of him. She started screaming and he kneed her in the face.

He then made her lie down, and kicked her again in the face. She remained there for a minute or two. He then ordered someone to open the main door. He dragged her by the hair and she stood up. I saw him take her towards the door.

This time I did not see the actual shooting. I heard a shot and then saw the body falling on the platform. The accused ordered two passengers to throw her off the stairs. One of those ordered to bring the girl forward and throw her off the stairs was Ashraf, a security guard. I do not know who the other man was.

In desperation I called the tower. "Another passenger has been executed. Please do something about it."

At the word execute, the courtroom seemed to draw a collective breath. It was the first time anyone had used that word so far in these proceedings.

Defense Counsel Dr. Joe Mifsud asked that Captain Galal be required to withdraw while he spoke to the Magistrate on behalf of his client, Omar Rezaq.

Defense Counsel said, "Witnesses should say only exactly what happened. If there was a shooting they should say that and not say execution. Using the word execution is expressing an opinion."

Magistrate Dr. Gino Camilleri cut in. "The witness was describing in his own words what he saw."

The defense persisted. "We ask the Court to enter a note in the transcript saying that the Defense objected to the use of the word "executed." In its meaning the word "executed" not only describes an exterior fact but also implies in a certain way a willful homicide. Witness is not competent to say what was behind the action."

The Court rejected the request by Defense. Captain Galal was asked to return to the stand and continued with his testimony:

In both shootings the lights inside the aircraft were on. Up until the second shooting, the lights on the tarmac outside were on. The accused returned to the cockpit and we started negotiating again. These negotiations continued intermittently during the time in Malta.

"Order them to send fuel," he demanded once more.

I sent his message and waited with the usual misgivings for the answer. This time it was a more positive "no" but I did not reveal that to the hijacker.

"They say no fuel will be given now that you are shooting passengers."

He did not answer. I tried another approach.

"If you stopped the killings and let the passengers off, you'd still have control of the aircraft and could go where you wanted. They'd give you fuel if the passengers were safe."

"Why should I trust them to do that?" he snapped.

I tried again. "They say the best thing for you to do is give yourself up."

"I will never surrender."

"They say that at least in Malta your life would be guaranteed. There is no death penalty here."

"I will never surrender."

"They say that Malta sympathizes with the Arab cause so it would be safer to surrender here."

"I have no intention of surrendering."

It surprised me that he never asked the other hijacker what he wanted to do.

"I want to speak to the Algerian and the Libyan Ambassadors," he said next.

I informed the tower.

"There is no Algerian Ambassador in Malta," they said. "But the Libyan Ambassador will be on his way shortly." They added, "There is a PLO representative available."

"I do not wish to speak to the PLO."

About then I saw the third hijacker for the first time. With the one having been killed there were only two hijackers left, the one in the front and the one at the back. He came into the cockpit and told the accused he had seen military vehicles at the rear of the aircraft.

I was glad of the interruption by the third hijacker. I had been desperately dragging out the conversation with the accused to keep him from executing another passenger.

After the third hijacker returned to his post at the back, I once more asked their demands. "If you will tell me your demands I will put pressure on the Egyptian authorities to see if they can get the Malta authorities to give you fuel."

"My demands will come later," he answered shortly.

It was about an hour since the second shooting and the accused was getting restless again. He made a move to go out to the passenger cabin once more and I asked if I could go with him. He refused.

The door of the cockpit had been open for some time now and I had been able to get glimpses of what was going on in the cabin. At one point I had noticed that the passengers had been given a new seating arrangement. It appeared that certain nationalities had been placed together in the front rows. I had seen three people, a tall man and two girls who appeared to be Americans, moved into a seat together near the front. From the way they walked it appeared that their hands were tied behind their backs.

I heard the accused threatening someone. "If you don't tie the knots well I will tie you up instead."

I was still trying to think of something I could do to delay the killings when I saw the accused waving his gun at the tall man and my heart sank. The man, he appeared young, was quite calm as he moved from his seat into the aisle.

He walked towards the entrance door followed by the accused. Behind them were the two helpers who had dragged the second girl out to be shot. I wondered how they could do this.

For a time they disappeared from my vision and then I heard a shot. I saw the body falling on the platform.

The two helpers dragged the body and threw it over the platform onto the tarmac.

The accused had given a deadline of 30 minutes on this killing but by talking I had managed to put it off for awhile.

This third shooting, of the American man, occurred during the night.

I once more contacted the Maltese authorities. "Please give us fuel. I am prepared to do anything but please stop the shooting."

The fourth one to be shot was a woman who I later learned was an American named Scarlett Rogenkamp. She had been sitting next to the man. She was a very brave woman. When the accused approached her she stood up and walked calmly with him to the aircraft entrance. Her hands were tied behind her back. With the woman and the accused were the same two helpers as in the previous shooting.

Again they disappeared temporarily from my vision, then I once more heard a shot and saw the body fall face down on the platform. The woman was also thrown over the platform on to the tarmac.

There were no more shootings for the rest of the night.

In the morning I saw certain movements of military personnel. It was about 6 a.m. During the night the passengers' cabin lights had been switched off.

Soon after parking in Malta I had put the plane's lighting and air conditioning systems on the auxiliary power unit which had consumed the little fuel that remained. This was part of our emergency procedure.

I was now positive there was no solution for this crisis except for external help. We had to be stormed somehow, sometime, somewhere. So I pulled the circuit breakers of the aircraft's outside lights so that the accused would not be able to use such lighting to see any advancing external force. I did this after the third shooting, without the accused noticing.

Despite my efforts, the accused saw the soldiers and ordered me to ask the control tower who they were. The tower replied that it was a unit stationed there to protect the aircraft from being attacked by foreign forces. Accused told me to tell the authorities that those military personnel must be withdrawn or else he would explode the aircraft. At the time there were a few soldiers lying in the grass.

The soldiers retreated from around the aircraft. However, we kept seeing movements and accused again asked for someone who spoke Arabic. He continued to negotiate, this time through the prime minister himself.

Negotiations now took a different direction. The interpreter said that even if the plane were given fuel American planes would not let it go anywhere and that there were military planes in the area. He suggested that the best thing would be for the hijacker to surrender.

This time I saw the accused hesitate momentarily. His anger and nervousness also seemed to increase. He began threatening the guards he had been forcing to do his bidding and grew increasingly concerned about the movements outside the plane.

Finally he decided to go out the entrance door and have a look for himself at the rear of the aircraft. He took one of his "helpers," the security guard who had been in the cockpit.

Keeping a gun in the guard's side, the hijacker used him as a shield.

The first supply of food was delivered during the night. The same two "helpers" he had been using throughout the hijacking were ordered to pick up the food from the steps. When the accused had first said he was hungry and asked for food I warned him the food on the plane was not good and we would have to order some. It turned out to be a comparatively easy operation, perhaps because at that time the accused had not yet seen the movement outside the plane and under the cloak of darkness felt comparatively safe.

At about 9 a.m. the accused was again hungry and we went through the same operation. The white van drove up and two men alighted with a box of food. I had the megaphone in my hand and the accused told me to tell them to put the food on the steps. They put it on the first two steps and then moved to the side where the bodies had been tossed off.

The accused was furious. He stretched his hand out of the cockpit window and pointed the revolver at the two men.

"Stop! Stop!" I shouted through the megaphone. I was afraid he would shoot them too. They stopped and he withdrew his arm.

"Bring the food to the top of the platform," I said as calmly as I could.

They did as I asked them. The accused became involved with getting his helpers to open the door and bring in the food. From the cockpit I could see the men go to the side of the plane again. This time they picked up a body and put it in the van. Because they only did it once I assumed that under cover of the darkness, the soldiers lying in the grass had managed to move the other bodies the night before.

The stewardesses distributed the food to the passengers. The accused sat on the observer's seat munching a sandwich. He had removed his hood by rolling it up on his forehead. He did this periodically. I guessed it was because it was so hot. Sometimes when he rolled it up little bits of green wool clung to the sweat on his face.

About 10 a.m. while he was still eating he looked at his watch and said, "I am going to kill another one."

I said, "Is it a habit for you to kill after each breakfast?"

"There is a proverb among our people that death is merciful. Hijackers are prepared to die. They should be too."

"It is not an Egyptian proverb. It must be Palestinian," I said. I suspected that was his nationality.

"My father was a strong man, he used to drink olive oil," Omar remarked. I knew this was an old Palestinian feat of manhood.

"You are going to die," he said, "Because of your military service you will have a military funeral leaving from Omar Makram mosque in Cairo where formal funerals are held."

I wondered at his knowledge of Cairo and military funerals. I suspected he must have had some military training. I was aghast that he could kill so soon after eating. I was also wondering about his next victim. To delay it as long as I could I continued to engage him in conversation. I again asked him how much fuel he needed.

His answer was to ask me how many flying hours there were from Malta to Tunis, to Libya, to Algiers and to Damascus. I didn't know whether he was trying to put us off by mentioning these different possible destinations or if he, himself, was trying to decide where to go. I reminded him that the Libyan Ambassador might be arriving.

Some time before there had been a call from the tower from someone saying he was the Libyan Ambassador. The accused had taken the microphone and said "How can you guarantee to me that you are the Libyan Ambassador?"

"I've got no guarantee but I am the Libyan Ambassador."

"Well then come to the plane."

"Why?"

"Because I have a message to give you."

"Why don't you give it to me over the wire?"

"No, you have to come here to the plane."

"Wait a minute and I will consider it," the man who identified himself as the Libyan Ambassador replied.

I was using the potential arrival of the Ambassador as a way to delay the next shooting but it only saved minutes. After he finished his sandwich the accused said, "It's time for the shooting," and went into the cabin. It was shortly after 10 a.m.

I saw the same two men bring the woman from the third row where the man and woman I guessed were Americans had been seated. I couldn't help but think how dreadful it must have been sitting there waiting after her companions had been shot. But she appeared calm, perhaps resigned.

She too was taken to the platform outside the aircraft. Being daylight I could see the accused's hand with the gun in it. The woman came a little bit further out on the platform than the others. I could see this from the cockpit window. Her hands were tied behind her back with a man's tie.

The accused shot her in the back of the head. She fell face down.

I saw her being thrown over the platform onto the tarmac, this time towards the nose. As she fell she hit her head against the mobile passenger steps and left a large blood stain.

I could not take my horrified gaze away. I saw her fingers moving despite all the blood she was losing from her head wound. I was sure she was still alive.

This time I fairly shrieked through the microphone.

"Another woman has been shot!"

Apart from the shootings I have described and the shooting during the storming, there were no other shootings in Malta.

My co-pilot wanted to use the rear toilet. We got permission from the accused for him to leave. He looked more ghastly when he returned than when he had left. The next time the accused left the cockpit my co-pilot managed to tell me what it was like.

"I saw the other hijacker," he said. "I told him in Arabic that the toilet was full."

"If you want to use it, you have to fix it," he snapped.

"I don't know what it must be like for the passengers at the back," the co-pilot added. "The smell is terrible. But maybe they're too terrified to notice."

The accused stayed in the cabin for awhile now. I heard him ordering some women passengers to give him their handbags. He ripped off the straps and used them to tie the entrance door handles from the inside to the chute bar so as to lock them from the inside. The only door left untied was the front left entrance door.

I contacted the tower, ostensibly to request a toilet service car in case the accused returned and caught me using the microphone. I said in English, "Listen and listen good. I am not going to repeat this. I am not going to repeat this. To whom it may concern. The main doors are locked from the inside and the only access is through the overwing hatches. Over and out."

I did not expect a reply. The tower was extremely cautious and they never put me in a bad spot.

It was evening of the second day, about 9 p.m. Athens time, when I noticed a light on the control panel. My co-pilot noticed it too. We exchanged glances before he quickly turned it off.

It meant that the rear cargo door had been opened. Fortunately the accused was distracted by the tarmac lights which had just gone off and did not notice.

"Why have the lights been switched off?" he demanded of the tower. He had now mastered the use of the microphone.

"It is another procedure to protect the aircraft from being attacked," they assured him.

The accused was now sitting in my seat and I was on the observer's seat. He had suspected that something was going on and wanted to look outside from the cockpit window. He held a grenade in his left hand with his thumb in the ring of the safety pin. In his right hand he still held the revolver.

Perhaps five minutes later, there were gun shots. Not many, less than five I thought. They were coming from the left side of the passenger cabin.

The accused leaped to the entrance of the cockpit door, which had been slightly ajar. He kicked it open and screamed "Ithbat." It can have two meanings: "on guard" or "stand still."

An explosion now ripped through the aircraft from the rear.

The explosion blew the panel of the cockpit door inwards. Only the frame remained hinged in place. I leapt from the observer's seat and tried to grab the accused by the shoulders but couldn't quite reach him.

From the corner of my eye I saw the co-pilot jump out of the cockpit window. I knew he was following the drill I had given him during the night, standing on the seat to make it easier to get his feet out the window and then sliding down the emergency rope he would have tossed out. The blast did not cause any injuries to us in the cockpit. There was no shrapnel.

I managed to get to the cockpit entrance once the accused left it. He was dashing towards the aisle, holding the grenade high in his hand. I saw another hooded person run down the aisle toward him. I think "Ithbat" was meant as a warning for him.

As the hijackers met I saw the flash from the gun the second hijacker held and a bullet hit me. It did not pierce my skull but it forced me to my knees like a blow from a club. I hit my head hard against the back of the captain's seat. I thought I was dying.

There was a great deal of smoke in the passengers' cabin by this time. The first explosion had been almost immediately followed by a second, also from the rear.

While kneeling I grabbed the crash axe and struggling to my feet, I swung it in the direction of what I believed was the man who had shot me. I think I hit him somewhere between the neck and the head.

The axe I used does not really have a cutting edge but it is sharply angled on one side so that it can penetrate. The person I hit was wearing a hood. He staggered towards the rear of the plane. It was not the accused I hit. When I stumbled back to the cockpit after hitting the hijacker I looked through the cockpit window and saw the main door being forced open by two storming commandos.

Since I knew the main doors were locked and the terrorists could not leave through the emergency doors because the commandos were coming through those, I was sure the terrorists were still on board when I jumped out of the cockpit window. By that time the smoke had reached the cockpit and I was choking.

The last time I saw the accused he had a grenade in his hand and was running down the aisle.

When Captain Galal was called back for cross-examination he was asked to go into more detail about his description of the accused's behavior. It was obvious that the Magistrate, like the rest of us, had found some aspects of the accused's behavior rather strange.

It seemed to me that it would have been natural to expect even a killer to show some trace of emotion. But the accused never tried to justify anything. He was very calm after each shooting and on at least three occasions he whistled and sometimes he even hummed. The co-pilot and I talked about his behavior and agreed it was a very peculiar way to act, as if he had done nothing.

I have been a soldier and a hunter for most of my life and have never seen a creature that can commit murder so ruthlessly and mercilessly without showing any remorse. That's why I called him a "killing machine." I did not say he was "perfectly insane."

For the first time since Captain Galal had taken the stand he looked the accused straight in the eyes and repeated, "I would not call the accused insane because all his actions were deliberate. He knew exactly what he was doing all the time."

"Did you say the hijackers were singing and dancing?" the Defense Counsel asked.

"I said they did not go as far as dancing but they did sing."

"Captain Galal, we have some pictures of the corpses," Magistrate Camilleri said. "I'm sorry to have to show them to you. They are not a very nice sight."

"Thanks to him, I have already seen them – as they were that day," I answered, nodding my head angrily in the direction of the accused.

"Do you recognize, in this room, the person who entered the cockpit and told you the plane was hijacked?"

"He is the one sitting on the right. I can touch him if you want."

"I wouldn't advise it," the assistant to the Prosecutor said dryly.

Chapter 14

El Wakeel

The first passenger to escape after the Storming

<u>*From the Trial Transcript:*</u>

I am Mohammed El Wakeel. I am a catering school teacher. I was on the Athens-Cairo flight that landed in Malta. I was sitting in the midsection of the aircraft on the right. I was in the window seat, number F14 in a smoking area.

The passenger next to me was a sailor. We exchanged a few words as you usually do on a plane. I found out he was married with a grown son. I told him about my family. It was the normal put-in-time sort of conversation. Then I sat back to wait for the beverage trolley and a newspaper.

Suddenly I heard the man beside me give a grunt and he seemed to collapse on his seat. I peered over the seat ahead of me to see what had shocked him so.

Before I could quite figure it out, a man rushed down the aisle, pushing the hostess out of his way. At the front I saw a man with a pistol in one hand and a grenade in the other. He shouted in Arabic, "Anyone who moves I will shoot him."

By the time the shooting broke out in the air the man beside me was weeping and I was in a state of shock.

Sometime after we landed, I was moved from F14 forward to a seat close to the right-side emergency door. My companion moved with me. By now he was talking crazy, babbling really. He said, 'The telephone is ringing but I don't want to answer it because it is someone wearing red shoes."

I said, "It's all right. Don't answer it." I was trying to humor him and keep him quiet so as not to draw the hijackers' attention. The next time he said, "I won't answer it because it is my wife and she wants me to shave off my beard."

I continued to try to soothe him. Finally he jumped out of the seat and walked up to a hijacker. I heard him say, "I have just hijacked a plane and a passenger has died in my lap."

I held my breath. I expected the hijacker to shoot him, as he had already shot several passengers. I realized of course that it was the shooting of the passengers that had got to the man. It was bothering us all. But it was hard to believe that what had seemed a perfectly normal man could be changed into such a basket case in so short a time.

The terrorist didn't shoot him. He motioned one of the helpers who had been dragging out the passengers to be shot, to bring him back to his seat. I have heard that most people are afraid of anyone who appears crazy. The terrorist seemed to be no exception.

After the shootings and with this mumbling stricken creature beside me, I could stand no more. I looked out of the window and tried to shut out all that was happening around me. My nerves were completely destroyed.

When the storming began, I was lying face down on the floor. I had heard a big explosion. It seemed to be very near me. I thought it was a hand grenade although I did not see anyone throw one.

I had seen a head very close to the window and as soon as I saw this I lay down on the floor. I knew something was going to happen. It was still dark.

Immediately after I saw the head, commandos opened the emergency exit towards the inside. The door fell on top of me. I felt more than one person coming into the aircraft as they passed over the emergency exit, which was still on top of me. When I felt that there was no more pressure, I pushed the door, which was not a heavy one, away and ran outside.

At the time I was wearing a waistcoat, a shirt and a pair of trousers. I had taken off my jacket as I was hot and left it inside.

When I jumped onto the tarmac from the wing I was shot at and was hit twice. Shots were being fired all around. I was hit in my right forearm and in my right leg. I shouted, "Stop, I am Egyptian. I am a passenger."

After Wakeel testified, we in the courtroom let out our breaths as though we too had escaped from the plane. From the moment Dr. Buhagiar had taken us on that doomed aircraft we had watched as the hijacker killed passenger after passenger and dumped them from the plane. We had smelled the smells, watched the frightened passengers slowly disintegrate, breathed the dead air once the oxygen tank had run out, eaten the limp sandwiches, smelled the deadly smoke from the explosion and finally escaped with this first passenger to get out. With him, we too, gulped deep breaths of the fresh night air, ran from the terror, dodged the bullets.

But then like everyone who has been through a traumatic experience, we found ourselves inevitably going back to pick at it. First we were with the Police Special Mobile Unit as they recounted what they had seen and done.

Police Inspector Daniel Gatt testified first.

I went to the hospital to interview the passengers. I spoke to Patrick Scott Baker, the two Egyptian air hostesses and to the Egyptian sky marshall who was the first to be thrown on the tarmac.

The first woman who was certified dead was Scarlett Rogenkamp. The second was Nitzan Mendelson although they were not shot in that order. Nitzan Mendelson was operated on in an effort to remove the pressure from a bullet in her head. No attempt was made to remove the metal as it was too dangerous. She died on December 1st.

I discovered that Artzi Tamar had received two bullet wounds, one beneath her right eye and the other in her thigh. She was conscious. Apparently thinking she was in Arab country, she first claimed to be an American living in New York. She later admitted she was an Israeli.

The last one who was shot, Jackie Pflug, an American, had a bullet wound in her head.

There were 32 people in the hospital including those who were admitted before the storming. Among these were four Egyptian soldiers and a Maltese fireman.

Police Inspector Cassar testified next.

I was instructed to recover the bodies under the aircraft. P.S. Zammit and I approached the aircraft from behind. The weather that night was awful. It had been raining since 11 p.m. and there was lightning. It was very cold.

We crawled on the grass from where our unit had been stationed earlier in the night. When we reached the tarmac we made a dash to get under the aircraft before we could be seen. Then we crawled under the fuselage until we reached the first body. The plane's undercarriage lights were on and there were also some lights on inside the aircraft. Thanks to these lights as well as the lightning I could see there were three bodies.

We approached the nearest person. He was face down. We turned him over and lifted him by the armpits. We crawled under the fuselage to the tail dragging this man with us. We tried not to cause him any more harm than had already been done. When we reached the tail, we stood up and quickly walked across the tarmac. We could not move as fast as we wanted to because he was a big man and very heavy. Whenever lightning flashed we hit the ground and remained motionless so that we could not be seen from the plane. When we got to the grass, other members of our unit put the man on a stretcher and carried him to the ambulance.

Two others of our group, Brincat and Callus, rescued the first woman. Zammit and I went back for the other woman. We brought each of them out in the same way as we had the man. However because they were not so heavy we could do it faster and without so much fear of being seen from the plane.

Warrant Officer Charles Mifsud was the last witness of that day to testify.

When the lights on Park 4 were switched off, that is when it was in total darkness, I saw someone approaching Major Borg and myself.

Major Borg called out, "Police, Police" but the person continued to walk towards us. Major Borg said "Stop" and the person put her hands up. She was wearing a pair of jeans and an anorak. She said, "I was a passenger on the plane. I need a doctor." She seemed upset but was not behaving suspiciously so we led her across the grass and put her in a car. "Keep calm, you are safe," we kept saying to stop her from shaking and crying.

The tension could almost be felt in the courtroom. The Police unit had described how four of the bodies had been removed from under the plane. The first, we knew, was the security guard who had been tossed off the plane soon after it landed in Malta. The woman who had walked away was, we all now knew, the first Israeli girl to be called out, Artzi Tamar.

The two women dragged away were the second Israeli woman shot, Nitzan Mendelson and the first American woman shot, Scarlett Marie Rogenkamp. The caterers had taken away one woman, presumably Jackie Pflug. There was only the American man, Patrick Scott Baker, whose escape from under the plane had not, so far, been accounted for.

The only testimony ever given by the accused, Omar Moham-
med Ali Rezaq, was to Security Superintendent Charles
Bonnello before the trial.

Bonnello: "Why did you shoot the Americans and the
                Israelis?"

Rezaq: "That is our principle. Israelis kill us on land,
                air and sea therefore when we meet them we
                kill them."

Bonnello: "Why are you against the Americans?"

Rezaq: "We are against Americans because they are
                imperialists and Zionists. I do not shoot all Ameri-
                cans. There are some who work for peace."

Rezaq's final direct testimony was "I did not expect to go to
hospital. I expected either success or death."

Chapter 15

Patrick Scott Baker

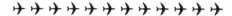

The only male passenger and the first American shot.

From the Trial Transcript:

At 10:07 a.m. March 24, Patrick Scott Baker took the witness stand. He said he was born and resided in Seattle, Washington.

"I am trained as a biologist and hold a degree from the University of Washington. I work in the fishing industry as processing manager. I am six feet five and a half inches tall. When the EgyptAir aircraft took off from Athens, destination Cairo, I was on Seat F Row 6 on the starboard side next to the window.

Take-off was normal. While in flight, about 25 minutes after take-off, I was reading a book when I noticed a man standing in the aisle at the front of the aircraft. This man was holding a revolver and a hand grenade.

I was scared and tapped on the shoulder of a Frenchman sitting on Seat D in my row. I pointed to the man with the gun. He looked over the newspaper he was reading and then went on reading again.

I couldn't believe he was taking it so calmly. Was he accustomed to this sort of thing? It was my first trip to Europe so maybe this wasn't as bad as it seemed. I decided to try to take it calmly too.

The man with the gun just stood there for awhile and then he started bodysearching the passengers.

He pointed at the passenger to be searched, indicating he was to go to him and with one hand still holding the gun he used the other to search the passenger. He also asked for their passports.

He would say things to the passengers as they were being searched. To a girl he said, "Welcome. You are French" and patted her on the cheek.

When the Israeli girls went forward to the hijacker they did not take their passports with them, presumably not to show they were Israelis. But they were made to go back for them. When he saw the passports he hit one of them in the head and made them sit on a seat in the front rows.

When I went up to him to be searched he asked, "Where are you from?" I replied "From America." He said, "But where from?" I replied, "Seattle, Washington." He told me to sit down after saying "Ah welcome."

I now sat on row 3A near the window on the port side. Sitting on the same three-seat row were myself, a Greek man, a French girl and a Spanish girl in that order [from the window to the aisle].

The Spanish girl was grazed by a bullet during the shoot-out. Later she picked up two slugs that had ricocheted. She wanted to keep them as souvenirs.

After the wounded air hostesses were removed from the plane, there was an announcement asking if there were other injured persons. I expected the Spanish girl to speak up but she did not, possibly to keep company with her French girlfriend.

It was a very turbulent flight to Malta after the shoot-out. I did not know we had landed in Malta. I assumed it was Beirut or possibly Tripoli.

Sometime after the Egyptian and Filipino women had been allowed off the plane, the hostess said "One Israeli girl please come forward."

I knew the girls because I had talked to them in Athens. Tamar stood up and went up to her. A little later I heard Tamar cry out "help." It was not a scream but something like a plead. I then heard a shot.

Tamar had been seated on seat 2A, in front of me. Seated on seat 2B was Nitzan. After this shooting Nitzan was very terrified and I tried to calm her down. About five minutes later the hostess called for the other Israeli girl. Nitzan covered her face. The hostess went down the aisle looking for her saying something like "Will the Israeli girl please come forward?" No one spoke.

The hostess went back to the accused standing in the galley area. They spoke in Arabic. The hostess then took a passport and went round the passengers to identify the Israeli girl. She identified Nitzan this way. She told Nitzan she must go forward but Nitzan refused.

Eventually two men brought Nitzan forward. They dragged her to the galley area. I could not see Nitzan but the Spanish girl told me that Nitzan was on the floor.

After the shooting of the Israelis I pretty much figured out that I would be dead soon. In other hijackings the Americans were always targets and I had not seen any other Americans on board up till that time.

The cabin lights were on all the time. I could see with the available light what was going on inside.

"I will be next," I said to the Spanish girl.

"Oh no," she gasped. "I can't believe that. They only shot those girls because they were Israelis."

"Americans are shot too," I said resignedly. "They have been in other hijackings."

The hostess came into the passengers' cabin with three American passports. "The Americans will please stand up," she said. I sat for some seconds wondering what to do and then I got out of my seat and walked to the galley area. There was no other place to go. There was a short, bearded man with a necktie in his hands. I knew he had been ordered to tie me up. As he did so, he said in English "I'm sorry." He made a gesture with his hands and head to show me that he was helpless.

After my hands were tied I was made to sit on seat 1D. Two American women were made to sit there too: Rogenkamp sat on seat 1E and Pflug on seat 1F.

Scarlett began crying. She said, "My hands are getting numb. They have tied my hands too tight. Can you get someone to loosen them?"

I suppose she asked me because I was in the aisle seat. I tried to attract the short man's attention but did not succeed.

"Work your fingers," I said. "That way they won't get so numb."

"Where are you from?" I asked after awhile. I was hoping to distract her from her hands.

"California," she whispered and then shook her head. I could see she didn't want to talk.

The accused motioned to the bearded man to escort me to the front door. The accused was standing, between the front door and the cockpit door. Subconsciously I had been waiting for this moment and trying to work out a plan of action. My first thought was to kick the accused and run out the door.

I stared straight into his eyes as I walked forward. And that was a mistake. From my look he seemed to sense what I was about to do and kept his distance. Defeated, I walked out of the aircraft. Accused had a revolver in his right hand and, I think, a hand grenade in his left. The short man held my left arm.

I walked to the edge of the platform. As I hit the top of the stairs my next thought was to jump. I glanced back and saw accused following me with the gun in his hand. The gun was pointed at my back. He was only about three feet behind me.

As I reached the head of the stairs and prepared to throw myself down I glanced sideways to my left to see where I would land. At that moment accused shot me.

It felt as if my head had been hit by a club. I could feel my head being thrust forward by the bullet. I could see stars for a split second. But I was still conscious. I decided to play dead and rolled down the steps in a summersault fashion. I rolled five or six steps. But that ruse didn't work either. Two men dragged me up to the platform again.

I had my eyes closed. It felt as if I were being lifted onto the rails. Then I was rolled over them and dropped straight down.

I hit something, I think it was the van and then dropped onto the tarmac. I lay there for two minutes or so with my back to the fuselage and facing the engine. I had landed on my back but then half-rolled face down.

My instinct was to run under the plane but I knew that if the accused was still at the door he could shoot me. From the shots I had heard I figured that was what had happened to one of the women. So I waited. Finally I couldn't stand it any longer, lying there fearing another shot. I scrambled under the fuselage where I felt I was finally out of range of the hijacker's gun.

I ran along the length of the fuselage towards the tail. When I cleared the tail I saw two men. Not knowing who they were, I ran at an angle away from them. I was sort of side-stepping to show them I was tied up so they would not confuse me with a hijacker.

One of them made what seemed like a friendly gesture and I ran towards them. They ordered me down on the ground.

"I am an American," I said. "They are shooting the Americans now."

How many hijackers are there?" one of the men asked.

"Two. One was shot in midair."

"Where are they on the plane?"

"One of them goes in and out of the cockpit. The other one stays mostly at the back."

I knew they must be working on a rescue plan, so gave them as much information as I could about the layout of the plane. When they had finished questioning me they radioed for an ambulance. One of them untied me and we ran to the ambulance which took me to hospital.

I never lost consciousness. Or if I did it was only for a split second after I was shot at.

They showed me some photographs at the hospital. I recognized one as the Frenchman who was reading the newspaper. The other I recognized as the accused. I recognized the accused mainly from his eyes and the shape of his face.

I spoke to the examiner but my eyes were on the man who had shot me.

Chapter 16

Jackie Pflug

The last passenger shot

From the Trial Transcript:

Dr. Zrinzo testified that on November 24 at about 3:20 p.m. he was asked to examine a Mrs. Jacqueline Pflug, a 30-year-old American. The woman was able to speak and was fully conscious.

An examination revealed a hole on the right-hand side of her head. As a result she was unable to see anything going on to her left. There was a big bump under the skin where the hole was and she had lacerations on the face. An X-ray showed a piece of metal stuck in the bones of her head with many fragments in the brain. A CAT scan confirmed this and also showed some blood where the fragments were.

Pflug was operated upon and the metal removed from her head. She was flown to a medical centre in Germany on November 29 and then taken for further treatment in the USA. Her wounds were serious but not life threatening. I gave the metal removed from her head to a nurse in the operating room to be consigned to the police.

Jackie Pflug's testimony in the form of a rogatory letter was one that we reporters covering the trial were permitted to read. Oddly enough I had seen Jackie when I made the hospital rounds to report on the casualties. She was unable to talk, the nurses had told me. Her testimony was more informal than the others, possibly because she was not in the courtroom facing the accused.

From Jackie Pflug's Verbal Testimony:

I was born in Pasadena, Texas. I became a school teacher, specializing in work with handicapped children. I had two dreams, as a girl, to see the world and to live where it snowed.

I moved first to Norway and experienced snow. I then moved to Cairo where my husband and I both taught.

About three months after we were married, I went to Athens for a weekend, mostly to shop. On my way back, my worst nightmare began happening before my eyes.

I think I had sensed a tenseness from the time we first boarded the plane. One reason may have been that we were late leaving. As a result everything was rushed and confused. I noticed what seemed to be more security men around than usual. They were going through the luggage, putting their hands into our bags. I had never seen that done before. But even as I stood in line, watching them, I thought, "I could have a gun and no one would know." They were going through the motions but I did not feel they were being thorough enough.

I don't know why I had this thought about guns. Maybe it was a premonition.

I had talked with an Egyptian before I got on the plane. In the midst of our conversation we had both noticed the woman with the fair-haired child and had automatically made a move to help her as she struggled to get what seemed a lot of luggage up the steps. Before we could reach her, a stewardess had come forward to assist her. As I got on I noticed the stewardess had placed her in a front seat.

I still sensed uneasiness on the plane.

A man who turned out to be the accused got up and went to the bathroom. He left a briefcase on the floor in front of his seat. The flight attendant noticed it and asked whose it was. The man sitting behind the accused, who also turned out to be a hijacker, snapped, "Leave it alone." The stewardess looked startled at his sharpness.

A moment later he jumped up brandishing a hand grenade and a gun.

I put my head in my hands.

The hijacker saw me and came and hit me on the side of the head. He seemed possessed. "Are you scared?" he snarled. I said, "No." I was determined not to show fear.

The Egyptian I had talked to before getting on the plane saw that the hijacker was giving me a bad time and spoke to him in Arabic. They began to argue with the gun still beside my head. This was the hijacker who was later killed on the plane.

After the shooting started on the plane, panic set in. The Egyptian went into prayer. I heard a baby crying as the gas masks dropped down.

The stewardesses had been preparing a meal when the shooting started. In the confusion and the turbulence as we came down, the doors of the cabinets flew open, there was food hanging out and some on the floor.

The panic seemed to go away once we landed. People talked to one another. Scarlett talked to a man from Belgium. They compared travel notes, mentioning places to go in Athens.

When the Malta officials said they wouldn't supply the fuel, the hijackers said they would execute someone every 15 minutes. That was when panic returned.

From then on they moved us several times. The FBI told me this was not unusual. They do it because they don't want the hostages to conspire against them.

The man from Belgium could see everything from his seat. I heard him say, "Oh God, they're shooting her again." Every time she moved they shot her again. I thought, "Why doesn't she just lie there? She might stay alive if she did."

They moved Scarlett and Patrick and me to the front. I had a choice of which of the three seats to take. My first thought was to take the aisle seat so I wouldn't need help to get in as I would if I was in the centre or at the window. The reason I would need help was because by then our hands had been tied with the neckties. As I hesitated a voice inside of me seemed to say, "Take the window" so I did.

As we sat there the accused kept coming out of the cockpit with a mask on. He kept looking at us, staring us down. It was bothering Scarlett so I whispered, "Don't look at him," and turned my own eyes away.

As they shot Patrick, I closed my eyes. I began to pray. Scarlett asked me what I was doing. When I told her, she asked me to say some prayers for her.

When they came for Scarlett, I again closed my eyes but I couldn't close my ears to the sounds. I heard the shots and the terrible thump, thump of her body as it hit the stairs and then the ground.

I prayed again.

Fifteen minutes went by, half an hour, two hours, three hours. It seemed as though my prayers had been answered. I had worked my hands free of the necktie but I didn't want anyone to know. The hijackers had allowed food on the plane by now. The stewardess offered to hold the food to my lips so I could eat. It was finger sandwiches. I shook my head, I couldn't eat. But I was thirsty. The stewardess held a cup to my lips so I could drink.

When the hijacker called me, I wrapped the necktie around my hands so they would think I was still tied. I didn't want them to be angry or hostile to me. I went up without crying or screaming.

He shot me. I felt heaviness. And next I felt hardness under me. I wondered if Heaven was hard and then realized it was the tarmac.

I lay perfectly still – remembering the girl who had been shot three times. I lay still for what I learned later was about five hours.

I had wanted to go to the bathroom on the plane. But I could not force myself to lift my hand and ask permission as the others were doing. I was afraid to draw attention to myself since I was the only American left. Now I relieved myself on the tarmac.

Finally some men came. The hijackers had had dark slacks and so did these men. I was afraid they were the hijackers so I made myself a dead weight when they picked me up. They tossed me on a pile of dead bodies.

As they drove away my body twitched involuntarily and someone said, "She's alive."

I expected another shot but when it didn't come I opened one eye and said, "Are you the good guys or the bad guys?"

The man answered, "We're the medics, honey. You're going to be OK."

I identified the accused from pictures shown me by the FBI in Washington where I have given this testimony.

Chapter 17

Tony Lyons

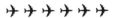

The passenger who believed he was next

<u>*From the Trial Transcript:*</u>

I was a passenger on the Egyptian flight from Athens to Cairo. On departure I sat in seat No. 2B. In seat 2A there was another Australian, a girl named Elizabeth Fisher. In seat 2C there was a man who turned out to be a hijacker. I recognize the accused present in this court as the one in seat 2C.

I was talking to Elizabeth when the accused rose from his seat. He was perspiring around the mouth and clenching his hands. I wondered if he was nervous about flying.

Elizabeth and I were still talking when she suddenly went very pale and said, "Is that real?"

"What do you mean?"

She nodded at the aisle. I turned round and saw the man who had been sitting in front of us standing in the aisle with a gun in his right hand and a grenade in his left. He had the pin through his teeth.

I don't know why but I said, "Are you having trouble?"

Through clenched teeth, he asked, "Where are you from?"

"Australia," I answered.

"You are welcome," he said. "Please move to the back."

One by one he asked people to rise and move down towards the rear of the plane. I put my hands on my head as he had ordered and walked to the back. Elizabeth Fisher walked behind me. When I got to the rear Elizabeth sat in the second last row of seats on the port side, the aisle seat. I had to clear the back seat on the port side of hand luggage. I sat in the last row, the window seat. In front of me was Elizabeth Fisher and next to her a lady, Valinda something. On her lap there was a child.

From my seat at the back I could not see as well as I had before. I saw the hijacker working his way down the aisle doing body searches. Suddenly I heard shots. I ducked my head and kept it down. About 30 seconds after the shooting the oxygen masks dropped down.

Everyone took one, including the hijacker at the back. He held the oxygen mask to his mouth. I wondered how he could use it with his hood on.

To my surprise he leaned forward and seemed to be trying to make sure that the baby on Valinda's lap was breathing.

Sometime later the hijacker at the back touched me on the shoulder and pointed to the rear toilet. I had been wanting to go to the toilet anyway so I got up at once and went in. It was when I tried to come out that I had trouble. When I started to open the door the hijacker waved his gun at me. I went back in and closed the door.

I was locked in the toilet for about half an hour. I tried to come out again but he pointed with his gun for me to stay in there. I heard some noises. It sounded as though the hijacker had placed some hand baggage outside the door. I did not try to come out again.

Eventually, I heard someone knocking on the door. It was a stewardess. She spoke in English and told me to move to the front of the plane. As I was moving up the aisle I heard someone shouting "Australia." I also heard them call out Row 2. I went towards this row and I noticed that the front area of the plane was taken up by passengers of Western origin.

When the first Israeli girl was shot, a stunned silence settled on the plane. It was as though everyone suddenly realized that although the shooting in the air had been understandable because two people were shooting at each other, this was different. This was murder.

The silence continued, broken only by the sound of crying.

When the second Israeli girl refused to walk the accused seemed angry but for the other killings he was calm at all times. He seemed to know what he wanted to do and he would do it with very little emotion.

After the death of the first American girl, there was no reaction from the passengers any more. It had become normal that someone was going to be killed.

During the night there had been a thunderstorm and hail was hitting the aircraft. We tried to sleep.

In the morning I realized for the first time that we were in Malta. About 10 a.m. we received some food. Soon after the accused came out of the cockpit and asked for the last American lady. She was taken to the front. I heard a shot and the sound of a body falling onto the tarmac.

There was a long period after that when nothing much happened. It was a time in which I wondered who was next. I had seen that my passport was put on the pile on top of the Americans.

"If there are no British," I thought, "I will be next."

Some food and water was distributed and I noticed that now when food came on board more people were allowed to move around on the plane than before.

Before the final terrible moments when the storming of the plane took place, I was trying to get some sleep. Not surprisingly, it wasn't easy. The smells, mostly from the rear toilet, were nauseating. There were sounds of muffled crying and moaning. I was trying to rest my head on the food tray but it wasn't comfortable. Every now and then I could hear someone calling in Arabic and the hijacker from the back would thump down the aisle and have a discussion with the one in the cockpit and then return.

This was making me very nervous.

Finally it was evening. It was dark in the plane and I again had my head on the table. I think I may even have dozed off for awhile until suddenly I was jarred wide awake by the sound of small arms fire. It seemed to be coming from several directions so I didn't think it was the hijackers.

Almost immediately I heard an explosion at the rear of the plane. It was a very large explosion because I could feel the pressure of it pass over me and then the immediate rise in temperature. The small arms continued. It sounded as though it was within the aircraft and the shots seemed to be coming too rapidly to be revolvers.

I kept very low in my seat to avoid the bullets. That may have saved me from the pall of smoke that settled around me. As I got the first whiff of it, I instinctively took a deep breath and held it. Eventually I could hold my breath no longer. I let it out and as I breathed in, I started to choke. I knew I had to get out of there. I could still hear shooting but now it seemed to be outside instead of inside the plane.

I jumped into the aisle. I couldn't see anything. I struggled to make my way down the aisle, gasping for breath. I stumbled over a body or something in the aisle. I got to where I thought the door was, still choking. The door was open. I fell out of it and on to the platform face down. I slid on my stomach down the stairs to the tarmac. I could not see anything, my eyes were burning from the smoke. I never saw the hijackers again until I saw the accused in hospital.

I was asked to come to give evidence in Malta by the Australian High Commission. At first I could not come because of my wife's health. She was very upset about what could have happened to me. However when I went through the questions in the copy of the letters rogatory, I noticed there were some inaccuracies in what I was supposed to have given as evidence whilst in hospital in Malta. It was not correct. I had to come to make sure the evidence I gave was correct.

In this evidence which I have just corrected and confirmed I testified there was a person who was seated next to me in seat 2C and who engaged in conversation with the stewardess – this is the accused.

The hijacker who came in and out of the cockpit and gave the orders is the accused.

The one who was killing everyone in cold blood and seemed the leader of the gang is the accused.

"You stated in your evidence that you were taken around the hospital to see passengers?" Inspector Gatt interjected.

"Yes, I was shown round first by the police on the morning directly after the storming of the plane around 3 a.m. I identified a man in one of the hospital beds as the accused."

I later told other people that I had seen the accused in the hospital. One of those I talked to was a Canadian who had lost his wife and child.

Abram: I had seen Tony Lyons in the hospital when I was getting stories for my newspaper. I had seen him talking to the man I later learned was a Canadian and had lost his wife. The Canadian seemed more distraught than the others, actually he seemed dazed. When I learned the loss he had suffered, I understood why.

We talked for awhile. I gave him what information I had. And then he said something I have never forgotten.

"She lost all her memories," he muttered. "And Andrew never had time to make any memories."

"Valinda had a thing about memories," he continued. "She had a habit of dragging them out at the oddest times. But mostly of course when she was lonely."

'I was born in harvest time,' she'd say. 'Have you ever seen a harvest moon? It gets so bright and clear and BIG in that big, big sky, that you almost expect to see the footsteps of the astronauts on it.' Another time she'd say, 'Have you ever heard the sound of a breeze through ripe grain, or the clicking sound of a grasshopper as it hits the grass, or seen the leafy shadows of a cottonwood across the lawn?'"

"She lost her memories, our memories."

I hoped my Canadian friend was not still hurting as he had been that day in the hospital.

Chapter 18

Dr. Abela Medici

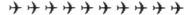

Forensic experts are the first to go back on the plane

From the Trial Transcript:

Dr. Abela Medici noted in his report that since heavy smoke was still coming out of the aircraft and firemen were still pumping water into it, neither the doctors nor the forensic experts would go inside.

In the meantime, Dr. Abela Medici had made arrangements for a temporary morgue at Luqa and Air Malta had offered a large hangar which was known as the Engine Shop.

The salvage of bodies from inside the aircraft continued until late in the night when at 2 a.m. on November 25 it was suspended. It continued at about 7 a.m. later that morning and was completed by that afternoon.

Some members of the forensic team collected the clothes of the people who had been admitted to St. Luke's. Dr. Abela Medici identified the bodies. To do this he sought the help of relatives brought to Malta for this purpose, referred to documents, seamen books and photographs which the dead carried on them and also found help from other medical experts.

The pharmacist, Mr. Hilary Aquis, helped Dr. Medici salvage the valuables from a number of corpses. Some seat supports had to be stripped to free some bodies which were trapped under the seats.

The bodies of four men, three women and five children were recovered from the airliner on the morning of November 25. One of the women recovered still carried her child who was breast-feeding. There were also two females in an advanced stage of pregnancy.

Five fingerprint experts were called as witnesses. Sergeant Vella gave the details.

"On Nov. 26 we first took the prints of a number of people found inside the aircraft. It is not always possible to take the fingerprints of the dead. In some cases only prints of two fingers could be taken as the others were not in a good state."

"Was this because of the fire burns, Sgt. Vella?"

"Yes, although in a few cases there were other reasons. The hand of a three-year-old girl who was probably sitting on seat 16F, was found hanging with the aft cargo door. The girl probably lost her hand after the explosion had caused part of the passengers' main floor to cave in."

At this point, Dr. Joe Mifsud, Counsel for the accused, offered to exempt the forensic experts from reading their report to the court.

Police Inspector Gatt, somewhat grimly, declined. "I think it would be better if the report was read out fully."

"Items found inside the passengers' cabin," Dr. Abela Medici continued, "included cartridges, clothes, some of them with blood stains and bullet holes, a brownish-green hood made of wool and a burnt revolver with six .380 cartridges in it still not fired."

"Ten cartridges were found on the tarmac just behind the port wing. Also found were parts of human flesh and bones, blood stains, part of a human nail, a badly torn shoe belonging to one of the commandos, a comb and a dark-blue jacket with three live rounds of ammunition in one of the pockets. This jacket belonged to Omar Mohammed Ali Rezaq."

"How were you able to identify this jacket as belonging to my client?" Defense Counsel asked.

"The holes in the jacket were compatible with the wounds sustained by Omar Marzouki, the name he was using in the hospital. The jacket had also been previously described by several passengers as being worn by the hijacker in the cockpit."

Dr. Abela Medici said that the identification of the dead, excluding Nitzan Mendelson, took three days. Blood samples of the dead were taken. The forensic experts established that the aircraft sustained considerable damage inside. The passengers' cabin was extensively damaged by fire, particularly the overhead luggage compartments. Extensive damage to the flooring towards the rear indicated there had been an explosion in the aft cargo hold.

There were also signs of an explosion at the foot of the Air Malta passengers' steps leading to the aircraft's main door. These steps were damaged and a crater was noticed at the foot of these steps.

Dr. Abela Medici said that four Egyptian soldiers were seriously injured by the explosion from the hand grenade at the foot of the steps. There was probably an explosion right by the feet of one of these Egyptian soldiers and probably the bones and human flesh found belonged to this particular soldier.

"Dr. Abela Medici, is it known who threw this grenade?" Inspector Gatt for the Prosecution asked.

"There was only one explosion caused by a hand grenade. According to witnesses an Egyptian commando was going up the passengers' steps as the hijacker who had been in the cockpit was coming down. At the foot of the steps were another two commandos. This hijacker hurled a hand grenade at the commandos and it exploded right by the feet of one of the two on the tarmac. Co-pilot Emad Bahey, running away from the plane, was hit by the shrapnel from this hand grenade."

"There was no hand grenade explosion inside the aircraft."

"A firing line was used by the Egyptian commandos to set off their explosion at the aft cargo hold. It was 11.60 metres long and detonators and insulators were found connected to this firing line."

"We found three live detonators at the corner of the aft cargo hold. These detonators probably did not go off because they were shielded by the luggage," surmised Dr. Abela Medici.

"There was one explosion in the aft cargo hold. This was centred beneath or close to seat 17D," Dr. Medici continued. "The explosion in the hold appears to have occurred closer to the passengers' cabin than to the floor of the cargo hold. Fire which resulted from this explosion also damaged the fuselage."

"Although I can only speculate," Dr. Medici said, "I believe the explosion caused more damage than the rescue team anticipated. At least six seats out of rows 16, 17, 18 and 19 on the right side of the aircraft (Seats D-E-F) were completely destroyed and the others badly damaged. The wheel-housing compartment was also damaged."

"Actually the explosion caused a fireball which went into the passengers' cabin. It simply followed the path of least resistance and ended up damaging even the fuselage ceiling."

"There have been reports that oxygen, still coming out of the emergency oxygen masks, might have fuelled the fire," Defense Counsel Joe Mifsud interjected. "Is this true?"

"No. We checked the oxygen systems. There were two independent systems on the aircraft, one feeding the cockpit and the other feeding the passengers. When checked at Luqa after the storming, the cylinder feeding the crew was still filled with oxygen but the other one was completely empty. I am certain that by the time the aircraft landed in Malta the oxygen supply to the passengers had already been exhausted. It is not possible that there was still oxygen in the cabin when the storming occurred."

"In our opinion," Dr. Abela Medici concluded, "the vacuum caused by the explosion as well as the lack of air inside the passengers' cabin suppressed the fire and rather than a blazing fire the explosion caused a large amount of poisonous smoke. This smoke caused the death of most of the passengers."

"Were you able to identify all the people on board the plane?" Police Inspector Gatt for the Prosecution inquired.

"We believe so. A fireman found a white plastic bag containing a number of passports. However these did not amount to the number of passports of all passengers on board according to the manifest."

"I compiled a 16-page list containing the numbers of the passports found and the names and dates of birth of the holders." Dr. Abela Medici added, "We had the most difficulty identifying the three hijackers since little was found on board the aircraft to help us."

"A boarding pass found in the jacket pocket of Salim Chakore showed that he was assigned Seat 4A. He was between 25 and 30 years old and spoke both English and Arabic. He had dark eyes and short, curly hair. The post-mortem showed he was 178 centimetres tall without shoes on. He wore a three-piece grey suit and a grey tie when he boarded the plane. When his body was taken out of the aircraft he was only wearing trousers and a tie. His jacket and waistcoat were found on the attendant's seat along with a light blue shirt. Chakore was wearing short boots and red bathing trunks [underwear] with blue patterns. He also had grey socks on."

"According to some passengers he acted very nervously and was very cruel and tough with the passengers. He carried a black revolver with a short muzzle and a hand grenade. He did not wear a hood."

"It was Chakore who ordered the collection of the men's ties. At the beginning of the hijacking he carried a white plastic bag containing ammunition. He also carried a brown attache case."

"In his pockets were found a lighter with the astrological sign of Aries and the date 21.3.24 engraved on it. He had a felt pen."

The money Chakore carried, the court was told, amounted to 5,050 Greek drachmas. His revolver, passport and air ticket were never found. Salim Chakore, the hijacker to die in the air, had five shots in him, four bullets remained inside him and the fifth passed right through his leg, leaving his body.

Bou Said Nareddin, the hijacker found completely inciner-ated at the back was on seat 1A at the time of the boarding. He had a moustache, was between 35 and 38 years old, had black hair, an aquiline nose and was of average stature. At least eight passengers said Nareddin wore spectacles. He was 165 cm tall.

Passengers described this man at the most kind of the hijack-ers and a "gentleman."

He also carried a white plastic bag and a brown attache case. He wore a mask all the time. While in Malta he went to the cockpit several times. This could account for the different mark-ings the ballistic experts found in the bullets removed from the passengers who were shot by the hijackers.

Dr. Abela Medici explained, "It is my belief that the accused and Bou Said exchanged revolvers at least once. This probably happened in the middle of the shootings which would explain why the two American women, Scarlett Marie Rogenkamp and Jackie Pflug, were hit by bullets with seven riflings to the right, the same type of bullets fired by Bou Said in the midair shoot-out. Bullets extracted from other victims, including Artzi Tamar, were copper guilded and had six rifling grooves."

After the shootings were over, Bou Said again went to the cockpit and this time got back the revolver he had originally had. A hand grenade was found beside Bou Said's body.

A post-mortem on Bou Said Nareddin revealed no bullets in him. This man was possibly hit by shrapnel after the explosion and there were indications that he may have lived for some time after the explosion by the commandos.

The hijacker who was in the cockpit (the accused) originally sat on seat 2C. Seated next to him was Tony Lyons, an Austra-lian, who came to be known as the one who believed he would be shot next after the Americans.

"In the row where the accused was sitting, sealed sachets were found on seat 2A in a bag which also contained a badge of the Palestine Liberation Front," Dr. Medici continued.

"We suspected these might contain drugs but it was only potassium aluminum sulphate, normally used as a mouth wash."

"This hijacker," Doctor Abela Medici said with a slightly embarrassed look at the accused, "is, we believe, 29 or 30 years old, has dark eyes, a long face, black hair, a long nose and is of average stature."

"He wore a dark blue jacket, light grey trousers, a white shirt, a slip-on and light-colored socks. Some passengers said he carried a raincoat on board. In his trousers' pockets were found ten notes of 100 dollars each."

"According to passengers this man looked very excited at first but became calmer later on. He carried a black revolver with a short muzzle and a hand grenade. Sometimes he wore a balaclava. He was described by passengers as the leader and a Palestinian with a Syrian accent."

"This man wore a green bathing costume [underwear]."

Dr. Mifsud said, "What relevance do the clothes of the hijackers have that you must go into such detail?"

"The clothes of the hijackers were particularly important because in them we found their boarding cards as well as the amount of money they were carrying." Dr. Medici added, "The accused was carrying one thousand dollars in American money."

Defense Counsel said, "I must again ask the relevance. What difference does it make, how much money he had?"

Inspector Gatt, the Prosecutor, interjected, "I think it has a lot of relevance, not least that it was American money."

Dr. Mifsud tried another tack. "Were all the belongings and the money of all the dead passengers collected as well? And was *their* underwear noted? What is sauce for the goose is sauce for the gander you know."

"What we have done is in accordance with the way other hijackings have been handled," Inspector Gatt answered.

Magistrate Dr. Camilleri concluded this exchange by saying, "The Court will decide whether the American money which the accused carried has any relevance to the case. And as the

Defense knows there is always the possibility for him to file an application to the Court about the matter."

"Dr. Abela Medici, have you ascertained how the commandos could set their explosives without being detected?"

"My first answer would be that the pilot and co-pilot by shutting off the light signaling the opening of the cargo area before the accused spotted it, was possibly the most important factor. It could also be that the hijackers after holding the plane for some 18 hours without incident had grown complacent. They were probably also tired from the long siege and therefore not as alert as they had been at the beginning."

"As I have recounted the commandos managed to install their firing line, about two kilograms of explosives, inside the baggage hold. To do this they had to remove some luggage. Eight pieces of this luggage were found on the tarmac after the explosion. Among them was a pushchair belonging to a Canadian baby who was on board with his mother. Another piece was one of two Egyptian canvas bags containing Diplomatic mail, en route from Canberra, Australia to Cairo. The other one was found on the plane. Although its outside casing was burnt, its seal was still in place."

"There were some things we found which we had difficulty explaining," Dr. Abela Medici acknowledged. "For example, on the ceiling above the captain's seat, were the words 'God Is The Greatest' in Arabic. Neither the pilot nor the co-pilot appeared to have noticed this being written. Perhaps it happened about the time of the shoot-out in the air when the pilot was absorbed in the emergency descent. The words must have been written by the accused since he was the only hijacker in the cockpit."

"Some pins were found imbedded in some of the corpses. We could only conclude they were blown out of the passengers' service units by the force of the explosion."

"We still haven't solved the third anomaly. A message in Arabic was found written on a sickness bag. Thinking the words might be an important message about the hijacking, we examined the script. It was signed 'Omar' but consisted of a message destined for the writer's wife and family. The message also contained a last will. Efforts are still being made to compare the fingerprints found on the bag with those of one of the dead."

"Finally, there was the question of why some passengers believed they had heard an extra shot when Nitzan

Mendelson's turn came. We believe that just before the hijacker shot Nitzan Mendelson, he noticed some movement from Artzi Tamar who had been shot first and was lying on the tarmac. He apparently aimed another bullet at her."

On November 28, after all the bodies had been removed, the fingerprint experts were sent to Luqa airport to examine the aircraft.

"Since the cockpit was the only part of the plane not touched by fire we decided that any possible fingerprints of the accused would only be found there." Sergeant Vella said. "A plan of the cockpit was made and it was decided to use the hard evidence method. This meant placing large plastic bags around the cockpit."

"We found a fingerprint on the glass of the cockpit's left sliding window. Since it was impossible to lift the finger print from the glass we removed the whole window and took it to the lab. Even there it was impossible to lift the fingerprint or photograph it. We applied dark powder on it to be able to lift it."

"No other fingerprints were lifted from the aircraft."

"We compared the print to those of the pilot and the co-pilot but the result was negative. In the meantime we had taken fingerprints from the people at St. Luke's hospital, among them those of Omar Rezaq."

"The fingerprint on the aircraft was the same as the small finger of the accused."

Dr. Abela Medici said, "There have been repeated references by the passengers to two people who helped the hijackers. In my opinion these two security men helped 'too much' [izzejjed]."

Ashraf Mohd Ibrahim was the security man wearing the pilot's uniform. The other three security guards were Hassan Elshershtawi, Nabil Farouk Zater and Medhat Mostafa Kamel.

Farouk Zater had wrapped a brown jersey around his pistol and the extra magazine and then pushed this jersey under the seat in front of him. This may have been why he escaped being identified as a security guard by the hijackers.

Mostafa Kamel carried his pistol and the extra magazine on him and it was he who shot Salim Chakore in the air. In all seven cartridges and six bullets from Mostafa Kamel's pistol were found.

"Although they were threatened by the hijacker on occasion, it may still be wondered, since they were being paid to guard the passengers, why they were so helpful to the hijacker."

Inspector Gatt for the Prosecution said, "I am sorry to put you through all this again Dr. Abela Medici but could you please give us an overall picture of how you have pieced this hijacking together from your evidence."

"I will be glad to, sir. EgyptAir's B737 arrived in Athens an hour behind schedule. At least two members of the crew said that an airport employee boarded the aircraft to clean the main cabin. They admitted this was done rather hastily."

"Among the passengers were 16 people, 13 of them Palestinians with Egyptian documents who arrived in Athens on Nov. 23 on a Libyan Arab Airlines flight. They were scheduled to take an Olympic Airways flight to Cairo but this flight was cancelled so they were transferred to EgyptAir's B737. Only two of these 16 passengers survived. They said they had not seen any of the three hijackers in the transit lounge at Athens."

"There were 27 shots fired during the shoot-out in the air."

On November 24, the day of the storming, the sun set at 4:50 p.m. The Egyptian commandos had flown in on a Hercules transport military aircraft. Under cover of the early darkness, two commandos managed to open the cargo door and as described, remove some of the luggage and place their explosives. We established that there was one explosion in the aft cargo hold beneath or close to seat 17D.

At 8:10 p.m. the aircraft lights went off and commandos mounted the starboard wing and went inside through the over-wing emergency door. A window in row 14 was broken and a hand holding a pistol came in shooting at random in all directions. The bullets from the starboard side were high and hit no one except for possibly grazing Captain Galal's head.

"The port emergency door was opened and a commando emerged shooting a machine gun from near the door. These bullets killed one passenger, fatally wounded another and seriously injured three others."

"The commandos outside were shooting inside the aircraft at random. They could not see where they were shooting."

"A 13-year-old Palestinian boy was hit by a bullet in the head during the storming and died instantly. There were signs that he was hit before the first explosion took place."

"Three Filipinos, three Egyptians, a Greek and a Palestinian were hit by bullets during the storming. All but two, an Egyptian and the Greek, died. Although they had bullets in them, they in fact died of the smoke. Another four passengers were hit either by bullets or shrapnel outside the aircraft. One was hit by a bullet from a .308 high-powered rifle as he was lying on the tarmac. Pictures of him were carried in the local newspapers."

Before the storming started the Egyptian commandos had had a chance to get information from the passengers who were able to walk away from the plane.

They knew that there were only two hijackers left. They also had a description of them, particularly of the one in the cockpit. This one had been seen inside the cockpit and also seen on the passengers' steps by newspaper reporters.

A commando had scaled a lighting tower in front of the aircraft and using a sniper rifle fired a shot at the cockpit. The bullet pierced the captain's chair which had just been vacated by the hijacker as he rushed out to the cabin to see what was going on. A few seconds earlier and the bullet would have killed him.

Suman Pablito, who probably escaped from the plane through the port emergency door, was hit by a commando bullet and as he, Pablito, was lying on the tarmac, he was hit on the head by shrapnel from the hand grenade thrown by the accused. This killed him.

The explosion in the aft cargo went off a few seconds later. A fire was started by this explosion and the fire caused toxic smoke which forced the passengers to run out of the plane. In the meantime the commandos, outside the plane, were shooting into the plane.

None of the commandos was treated for inhaling toxic smoke.

All the passengers who managed to escape the fire and the smoke were near the emergency exit at the time of the storming.

A total of 54 passengers died after suffocating from the smoke. These passengers could not leave the aircraft because of the shooting. Two of the 54 also had commando bullets in them.

Some children were found burnt in their seats. They were still in their seating position.

"The commando whose legs had been amputated by the grenade explained the instructions the commandos had been given."

"The first plan was to shoot the hijackers as the sniper had attempted. If that plan failed they were to explode the plane, at the cost of killing all the passengers."

In all 57 people were killed by the commandos. Three were directly killed by the hijackers.

Chapter 19

Committed for Trial

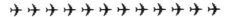

From the Trial Transcript: During the afternoon sittings on May, 26, presiding Magistrate Dr. Gino Camilleri read out a request from the Civil Aviation authorities for the hijacked plane to be removed to another site at the airport.

Both the Prosecution and the Defense did not find any objection to the removal of the aircraft from its present location on condition that nothing would be altered and that all precautions would be taken to leave the aeroplane in its present state.

The Court upheld the request and authorized the Boeing 737 be removed from its present location and placed on the side of Park 4 at Luqa Airport as indicated in the plan submitted in the application.

Magistrate Camilleri did not bring down his final decision on the hearings until April 3, 1987. The final testimony had dealt mainly with "housekeeping details."

The Prosecution asked for time to submit more questions for the rogatory letters to be sent to Anthony Lyons and Ahmet Fouad.

"We have already received answers to the rogatory letters sent to Jackie Pflug and Artzi Tamar. The testimony for Jackie Pflug was taken by judicial authorities in the United States and that of Artzi Tamar by judicial authorities of Israel."

"How many letters were sent out?" Magistrate Camilleri asked.

"Six in total. We have had the testimony of Jackie Pflug read into the transcript and Anthony Lyons came to Malta to give his testimony in person. The only other one we have heard from is Artzi Tamar. Do you wish her testimony to be translated and read?"

"If the Prosecution agrees, I think we can accept the Israeli woman's testimony and that of the Spanish and French female passengers, if they are received, as read in the presence of the accused," Defence Counsel Mifsud answered.

"The testimonies must be translated into Maltese and kept on file," Dr. Camilleri ordered, "but they need not be read to court." He added somewhat wryly, "The records of the case have already filled nine volumes."

Defense Counsel Mifsud asked to be heard. "I requested the assistance of the American Embassy in Malta in preparing my client's case but they did not wish to get involved on the advice of the US Department of Justice. I was finally able to make contact with the Maltese Embassy in New York through Mr. Alfred Falzon."

"The accused does not wish to put questions to the witnesses from France, Egypt, Israel and the USA at this time but he reserves the right to question them, if this is needed, at a later stage," Defense Counsel Mifsud declared.

"There is also the possibility the accused may want to be represented by a suitable person should he wish witnesses abroad to be questioned."

"In each of these instances the Defense requests that all expenses incurred in this regard should not be charged to the accused, especially in view of his being assisted by a legal aid lawyer."

Magistrate Dr. Camilleri answered, "It is my decree that all expenses in this regard will be paid by the Maltese Government."

Professor Joseph M. Ganado asked to be heard. "I wish to inform the Court that I have been contacted, by telex, by the heirs of Israeli Nitzan Mendelson. They have asked me to represent their interests in the case, in line with article 422 of the relevant law."

Dr. Joseph Mifsud got to his feet. "On behalf of the accused I wish to point out that article 422 refers to the rights of the injured party. The Mendelson heirs are not the injured party."

Magistrate Dr. Camilleri informed the Defense Counsel that Prof. Ganado's request would be entered in the records but advised him to make a formal request to the Court.

The Magistrate added, "Translations of the post-mortem examination of Nitzan Mendelson and Scarlett Marie Rogenkamp into Maltese have not yet been made. The Prosecution requests that those translations be made as soon as possible."

Forensic expert Dr. Abela Medici was the last witness to be heard. His bit of "housekeeping" had to do with newspaper coverage at the time of the bombing.

"Inspector Gatt gave me five negatives of pictures taken by Union Press photographers showing people standing on the aircraft's passenger steps. The photographs were probably taken on November 24, 1985."

"One of these photographs was first published by the news media on November 25 with a caption saying that a man could be seen shooting another person, namely a woman."

"The picture in fact showed a man dumping rubbish from the passenger steps on to the tarmac," Dr. Abela Medici said.

Magistrate Camilleri said, "The time limit in connection with the compilation of evidence is again running out. We have already had several extensions."

"The Prosecution has no further proofs to submit," Prosecutor Gatt said.

"The Defence reserves the right to submit its proofs at a later stage," Dr. Mifsud answered.

Magistrate Dr. Camilleri rose. "I now declare that there are sufficient grounds why the accused Omar Mohammed Ali Rezaq should be committed for trial."

Sentence

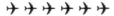

Omar Mohammed Ali Rezaq stunned a Malta courtoom when he pleaded guilty to seven charges, including two murders in connection with the November 23, 1985 hijacking in Malta.

Valinda Lenoard and her son Andrew were among the 54 people who died. They died of smoke inhalation. Since they were at the back of the plane where the explosions hit first they probably died very quickly.

After a two-day trial, Rezaq was sentenced to the maximum 25 years in prison.

From the Seattle, Washington *Register Guard*, July 17, 1993:

Suspect charged in '85 hijacking

WASHINGTON – A suspected member of the Abu Nidal terrorist group was charged Friday in U.S. District Court in Washington with air piracy in the 1985 hijacking of a flight out of Athens that ended in the deaths of 60 people when troops stormed the plane in Malta. Omar Mohammed Ali Rezaq could be sentenced to life imprisonment or death if he is convicted, according to Joseph Valder, an assistant U.S. attorney. Rezaq's attorney, Santha Sonenberg, an assistant federal public defender, said he would not enter a plea because the defense did not recognize the jurisdiction of the federal court in the case. Judge Royce Lamberth entered a plea of not guilty on behalf of Rezaq.

To the best of the author's knowledge, Rezaq has not been extradited to the United States at the time of this printing and is still imprisoned in a Malta jail.

Epilogue

It is eight years on November 24, 1993 since the fateful Malta hijacking. Eight times the Alberta snow has piled in winter drifts and melted in spring puddles on the grave where Valinda and her baby rest.

Ed has a new son and Harvey and Leah have three new grandchildren, granddaughters Quincey Jade and Sydney Paige and another little grandson, Chase Lindsay.

The farm where Valinda grew up looks the same. There have been good crops and bad crops since she last saw it. There have been dust storms and hail and rain – and the smell still blows off the feed lot. The flag still flies over the farmyard and inside the Uffelman home. Leah is, as always, ready with a cup of coffee and a chat around the family table.

The only room that is different is in the basement where the things that remind them of Valinda are kept – in particular the trunk full of cards and letters from across Canada and the United States expressing sympathy at Valinda's death. In this room also are the newspaper pictures, the newspaper clippings, the magazine articles and the tapes, one of them from Jackie Pflug and the other one a tape of the program based on Valinda's story which "Man Alive" produced. There too was where they took Valinda's luggage when it finally reached them, months after the hijacking. It was water-soaked and mouldy. "We had to destroy it," Leah says. "But I found a silk scarf that wasn't in such bad shape as the rest so I kept it."

Leah adds, "I sort of hoped once we received the luggage and took care of it, that there would be an ending somehow. But there wasn't."

"Valinda's death affected us all in different ways," Leah continues. "For the boys it has been as though they've gone through a tunnel and come out different men. Vance is a kinder, better man, I think. After he and Karen were divorced he married Debbie Kostrosky, nee Thurn and they live in the farmhouse where Valinda grew up. Debbie uses Valinda's old bedroom as her office. I think Valinda would like to know that the walls which held so many of her childish dreams now hold a computer, a telephone, a fax and all the other things that access the "outside world" she couldn't wait to enter. Vance told me the other day that he had stopped at the cemetery on his way home from Calgary. Perhaps it is part of his grieving. He and Valinda were not close and I think he regrets that.

Vaughn has been the slowest to reach the end of his tunnel. He was the closest to Valinda, the last one to see her so perhaps that explains why he became more aggressive, a little angry at life in the days after the hijacking.

However he is married now and he and Coreen have three children, our beloved grandchildren. He is a wonderful father. Recently, he has started going out more, has joined the ball team and is getting back into the community. The boys and Harvey all farm together. Vaughn and Coreen live on a property that the neighbors always referred to as "The Old Uffelman Farm." We used to call it the Tree Farm and that is where Valinda and the young people from Beiseker used to have their parties, their bonfires, their picnics. Valinda had a dream of building a house there sometime. She loved trees. If I believed in spirits returning to places they loved, I believe Valinda would have returned to the Tree Farm.

Verle-Ann has come out of it the best. Perhaps because of her own problems, she knew better how to cope. Her first training was as a hairdresser in Edmonton. She is now married to Randy Fewchuck, a sky-diving instructor. Verle-Ann helps him in his career, taking photos and videotapes as souvenirs for first-time jumpers. Her job skin is now only an unpleasant memory. Thanks to medical ingenuity, her ear has been replaced and by stretching her scalp, her hair now grows over the burned area. She wears her hair long and forward to hide the scars. Emotionally I think she is unscarred.

Harvey still wakes in the night sometimes and his anger and grief rush back again and he says, "If I could get hold of that hijacker, I'd kill him with my bare hands."

My last gift from Valinda was a gold chain. It has never left my neck since she died.

On December 2nd, 1985, the Valinda and Baby Andrew Leonard Memorial Fund was set up under the trusteeship of Eldon Knight, President of the Beiseker Lions Club, John Richter, then mayor of Beiseker and James MacLeod, broadcasting executive from Drumheller. Donations to the Fund not only came from neighbors and friends but from people such as Jack Daines of Innisfail Auction Mart, who devoted his advertising time to a woman he had never met. Proceeds from the fund are used each year to buy books for scholarship students.

Leah, Ed's daughter Chloe and Andrew on the Uffelman farm, with Valinda's pet horse

Ed went back East to work but makes frequent visits to the Uffelman farm. On his most recent visit, he brought his new wife Dorothy. They now have a son. Ed named him Alexander, a name similar enough to Andrew to have been emotionally chosen. It is also the name of Harvey's older brother, a well-known baseball player from Beiseker.

Ed and his new family now live in Mississauga, Ontario. Chloe and her mother are in Toronto so that Ed can continue to see his daughter. Ed's father Stan died of a heart attack.

"I have tried to forgive the hijacker – ever since Valinda's funeral I have tried, but I can't," Leah says. "I don't want to get caught up in hating, but I'm not sure I can avoid it. A man whose son was killed by a drunk driver once said he had forgiven the driver but in the next breath he said, 'God will get him.' I think that is how I still feel about the hijacker. 'God will take care of him.' "

"My one aching regret is that I did not 'listen' to Valinda the last summer she was home. That I was not more responsive."

"I remember her saying, 'You've no idea what I've been through' but I didn't give her a chance to tell me about it. I was too busy with the farm work. Summer is always busy on the farm. When Valinda, following me about the house, anxious to talk, lamented about the living conditions in Saudi Arabia, I said 'Two years out of your life is nothing. Think of the experiences you are having.' "

"If only I had known how few experiences she had left. If only I had listened . . ."

Finally . . .

✈ ✈ ✈ ✈ ✈ ✈

Valinda and her son Andrew are believed to be the first Canadians to die in an airjacking. Leah asked me to write the book so her daughter would not be forgotten. She also wanted it to be a reminder to Canadians that they are not immune to conflicts in the rest of the world.

Although I had never written a book of this sort before and wasn't sure I could, my daughter Susan and daughter-in-law Jan convinced me that I must. They too were the mothers of daughters and would not want them to be forgotten. To the best of my knowledge, except for the initial spate of articles (see Research Sources) little has been written about this tragic event.

So, to be able to write the book I visited Greece where Valinda and Andrew spent their final hours and met Kiki and Katerina, who had been the last to speak to them. My son Lorne accompanied me because in a chauvinistic world, it was easier for him to get information at embassies, newspaper offices and so on.

We flew from Greece to Malta in a plane similar to the hijacked EgyptAir 737. During the flight we were able to sit in various areas mentioned in the transcript, including the back seat to which Valinda and Andrew were moved. By then she knew she was in danger. What thoughts of Beiseker, of the farm, of Ed, had assailed her as she sat in those cramped quarters with a hijacker leaning over her shoulder? Sometime during the night had she scratched "ain't" in the grime of the window beside her? The burned-out hulk of the plane had been hauled away but we walked by the shed where the bodies had been laid out for identification.

Lorne went to *The Times*, Valetta's daily newspaper and found the reporter who had covered the story. After some discussion and after making Lorne promise not to reveal his identity, this man gave us the more than 200 pages of transcript. In my story I have called the reporter Abram (not his real name) and I have given him Jewish ancestry (which he does not have).

Why had we been able to get this transcript so easily when so many others, including Ed, had said they could get no information out of Malta? The reporter confirmed this apparent "Malta blackout" when he said he had not been allowed to print details of the trial in his newspaper.

So why now? Was he no longer afraid of terrorist retaliation? Could he no longer stand the frustration of "sitting on the story" as he had been doing for two years? His motivation remains one of those unanswered questions.

Whatever the questions, this was a book that had to be written. Paraphrasing of the transcript was necessary because as in most hearings so much of the testimony was repetitious. The only liberty taken in the book was in the chapter called "Jackie Pflug." Her official testimony was given in Washington, D.C. but there is no record of it in the transcript. During the writing of the book I prepared a set of questions which I used as the basis of a telephone interview with her. This interview plus a story published in *Family Living* and a tape sent to Leah, was used to reconstruct Ms. Pflug's testimony into the chapter format.

Research Sources	Interviews
Uffelman family papers	Leah & Harvey Uffelman
Beiseker's Golden Heritage	Ed Leonard
KIK Country	Sheila (Fischer) Felix
Chronicle of the 20th Century	Cindi (Ternes) Westwood
Saturday Night, Chatelaine	Cathy (Howden) Reboul
Alberta Report, Family Circle	Shelly (Schmaltz)
Calgary Herald, Calgary Sun	Schneider
Rocky View Five Village Weekly	Harvine Gilberg
The Times, Malta Review	Inga Kronlund
Athens News, Greek News	
Jackie Pflug	
Transcript of the Malta Hearings	